DEATH
OF AN
EX-MINISTER

Nawal El Saadawi was born in the village of Kafr
Tahla in Egypt. She trained as a doctor of medicine
and rose to become Egypt's Director of Public
Health. She began writing 30 years ago, producing
novels and short stories and in 1972 published her
first study of Arab women's problems and their
struggle for liberation, *Women and Sex*. She has
suffered at the hands of Egyptian censors being
forced to shift publications of her work to Beirut, and
earning her dismissal from the Ministry of Health.
She writes in Arabic but has published several
books in English, including *Woman at Point Zero* and
The Hidden Face of Eve.

By the same author

NON-FICTION

The Hidden Face of Eve
Memoirs from the Women's Prison
Women and Sex
*My Travels Around the World

FICTION

Woman at Point Zero
God Dies by the Nile
Two Women in One
*She Has No Place in Paradise
*The Fall of the Imam

DRAMA

Twelve Women in One Cell

*Available in Minerva

Minerva

DEATH OF AN EX-MINISTER

Nawal El Saadawi

Translated by Shirley Eber

Minerva

A Minerva Paperback
DEATH OF AN EX-MINISTER

First published in Great Britain 1987
by Methuen London Ltd
This Minerva edition published 1992
by Mandarin Paperbacks
Michelin House, 81 Fulham Road, London SW3 6RB

Minerva is an imprint of the Octopus Publishing Group,
a division of Reed International Books Limited

Copyright © Nawal El Saadawi 1987
Translation © Shirley Eber 1987

A CIP catalogue record for this title
is available from the British Library

ISBN 0 7493 9950 3

Printed and bound in Great Britain
by Cox & Wyman Ltd, Reading, Berks

Contents

The Death of His Excellency the Ex-Minister

The Death of
His Excellency
the Ex-Minister

Put your hand on my head, Mother, and stroke my hair and neck and chest gently, just as you used to when I was a child, for you're the only one I have left and your face is the only one in the whole world that I see or want to see in these final moments. How I used to want you to scold me for not having visited you for five years. But you were not the only one I neglected. I neglected the whole world, including myself, my house, my wife and my friends. Golf, which was my hobby, I haven't played once during these past five years. Even my little daughter whom I loved so much, I haven't seen. My own face, Mother, I haven't seen my own face. As I used to rush out of the house, I'd take a quick look in the mirror, not to look at my face but to adjust the tie around my neck or to check that the colour of my shirt didn't clash with that of my tie. And when I did look at my face in the mirror, I still didn't see it. When I looked at the faces of people in the office or in the street through the windscreen of my car, I didn't see them. If they spoke to me, I didn't hear them, even if they spoke loudly. The loudest hooting from any car, even if it was directly behind me, I didn't hear. So often did a car catch me unawares that I stopped walking.

I was, Mother, like one who neither sees nor hears nor lives in this world. In what world was I living then? Is there any other world in which a person lives, apart from that of people, unless God has taken him? I knew, Mother, that God hadn't yet taken me because I didn't see my obituary in the newspaper. It's not possible for a man in my position to die like that, without a large and prominent obituary in the papers and a large funeral procession in which the leading statesmen walk, the head of state in their midst and the whole world crying. The scene used to move me so much, Mother, that as I walked in such awe-inspiring funeral processions, I wished that it was I in the box. But since I don't remember ever being inside that box and since I always used to walk along behind it, it follows that I am alive.

But I didn't live in the world in which you people live. I wasn't concerned with the matters that concern you, but with more important issues. My concerns were limitless and were more than my mind and body could bear. Sometimes my body would seize up and stop moving, even though my mind would continue. At other times, it was my mind which would seize up until it stopped thinking, while my body kept on moving and coming and going. It would go to the office and attend meetings and head conferences and receive official guests at the airport and attend receptions and travel abroad on official missions. When I saw my body, Mother, moving like this of its own accord, without my mind, I was amazed and even scared, especially if I was in an important meeting which demanded my concentration and attention. And the only really important meeting was one in which I was a subordinate . . . .

From the time I became a government employee, I hated being subordinate. I got used to repressing my feelings of hatred before my superiors and would give vent to them only in my office with my subordinates, or at home with my wife, just like I saw father do with you, Mother. I was unable to express my hatred before my superior, even if he was an ordinary employee, like a head of department or a managing director. And what if my superior were not simply an employee, any employee of state, but the head of the whole state? What's that you say, Mother? Yes, my dear. I used to sit in my chair before him, my mind and body tense, senses alert and wide awake, fearful that he'd suddenly ask me a question to which I wouldn't know the answer, that if I knew the answer it wouldn't be the right one and that if it were the right one it wouldn't be the required one.

What's that you say, my dear? Yes, Mother. That's the ABC of politics which we learn in the first lesson. The right answer isn't always the required answer, but the required answer is always the right one. Men like us must always be alert, in mind and body, to distinguish the right truth from the wrong truth – and that's a tough job, Mother, tougher than any other in life. I had to sit in meetings, alert in both mind and body. I'd sit in my chair, my left hand lying in my lap, my right hand holding a pen poised above a sheet of paper, ready and prepared to pick up a gesture, any gesture, be it a nod of the head, a movement of hand or finger or a bottom lip tightening ever so slightly or a small contraction of a muscle around the mouth or nose or eye. I had to distinguish the movement of the right eye from that of the left. If I saw a movement the moment it happened, or even before it happened, I had to interpret it quickly in my mind. My mind had to be even quicker than me and interpret it before I did. My eyes had to be quicker than my mind and had to see a movement even before it took place. My ears had to be fast and hear a sound even before it was made.

What's that you say, Mother? Yes, my dear. During these important meetings I relied on my five senses. My mind and body were transformed, as I sat in my chair, into a mass of hypersensitive nerves, as if naked radar wires wrapped around each other were making my head and arms and chest and stomach work. I was so sensitive, Mother, that I would feel my stomach tremble as if it contained an electrical circuit, especially when I stood next to or near him. I'd feel the fingers of my right hand tremble, even though I'd clasp them with my left hand, with both the right and left pressed against my chest or stomach. My legs would also be pressed together, whether I was sitting or standing. That's how I was, Mother, when I was with him. My body was unable to adopt any other position. When the light fell on my face and the lens was focused on my body to photograph me for the people, I tried to release my right hand from the left and lift it off my chest or stomach, but I couldn't. I'd find them heavy, as though paralysed. What's that you say, Mother? Yes, my dear. That was the picture I saw of myself in the newspapers and I was ashamed. I tried to hide the paper from my family, especially from my young daughter who, with her little fingers, pointed to my face amongst the others in the paper and said to her mother, 'Isn't that Father, Mama?' And she, with the pride of wives of great men, replied, 'Yes, that's your father, my darling. Look how great he is, standing there with the president of state!'

My wife's voice rang in my ears and I realized it wasn't her real voice, that beneath the voice there was another that she had been hiding since time began and would continue to hide for all eternity, from the time we married until our death, hiding her real self and my real self in a deep and remote recess inside her. I sometimes felt it beneath my hand, like a chronic and hardened swelling which would not dissolve.

What's that you say, Mother? No, my dear. I was ashamed only in front of my little daughter, for even though her eyes are those of a child, perhaps for that very reason, they can always see through me and expose my real self which no one on this earth, not even I myself, can uncover. Do you remember, Mother, you always used to tell me that the veil was transparent for a child? I didn't believe you at the time, but I've realized since that sometimes, when my little daughter looked me in the face with those wide and steady eyes of hers, I felt frightened. At times I thought that this strong and steady look was not that of a child, especially not of a girl, or more exactly, a natural girl. The look of a natural girl, or even of a natural boy, ought to be less penetrating, less steady, less impudent, especially when directed at a larger and older person in authority. And what if this person is the father, master of the family and its provider, who works and who spends and whose right it is to be respected and obeyed by all the members of his family, big or small, especially the young ones . . .?

What's that you say, Mother? Yes. That's exactly what you used to tell me when I was a child. It has always stayed in my mind, to the extent that I used to tell it to my wife and repeat it to my daughter, and I'd even say it to those employees under my leadership or authority. I felt pleased with myself saying it, like a child pleasing its mother. I even felt admiration for myself, to the point of vanity, when I saw the admiration in the eyes of the employees around me, and I grew more confident that what I was saying was absolute truth for all eternity and that whoever said anything different was mistaken or blasphemous.

What's that, Mother? Yes, my dear. All my life, from the time I was a junior employee until I became minister, I could not befriend any employee who contradicted me. And that's why, Mother, I couldn't stand that woman, why I couldn't bear to remain sitting in my chair, keeping my normal composure, as dignified as any other minister in the presence of his employees. I could only bear it, Mother, by jumping to my feet and shouting with anger unusual for me, losing my dignity and my nerve, saying nothing meaningful, unlike what I was used to saying. I don't know, Mother, why I couldn't bear it nor how I deviated from my usual calm and dignity. I wasn't angry with her for expressing an opinion different from mine, or because she was a junior employee whose view differed from that of a minister, or because she was a woman holding her own opinion before a man, or because she called me 'Sir' whereas all the other employees addressed me as 'Your Excellency the Minister'. But I was angry, Mother, because when she talked to me she raised her eyes to mine in a way I'd never seen before. Such a gaze, such a strong and steady look, is daring in itself, even impudent, when it comes from a man. So what if it comes from an employee, from a woman? I wasn't angry *because* she did it, but because I didn't know *how* she did it, how she dared do it.

What's that? Yes, Mother. I wanted to understand how that woman did it. The desire to know took hold of me to the point of anger, anger with myself for not knowing and because I wasn't capable of knowing. Anger overcame me to the point that, the following day, I issued her with an order to come to my office. I left her standing before me whilst I sat and made her feel that she didn't exist. And I kept her standing whilst I sat talking on the telephone, laughing with the person who was speaking to me. The strange thing was she remained standing. She just didn't hear my voice nor did she look at me, but gazed at a picture hanging on the wall. I thought she'd look at me when I'd finished on the phone, but she kept staring at that picture on the wall as though I didn't exist. I tried to study her features before she moved and saw me, but she turned her head and her strong, steady eyes fixed themselves on mine. I jumped, as though all my clothes had dropped off me, all of a sudden. I felt ashamed; it reminded me in a flash of my little daughter's eyes. In one moment, the shame turned to anger and in another fleeting moment, the anger turned into the desire to shame her as she had shamed me. I found myself shouting in her face, in an unusually loud voice, 'How dare you? Who do you think you are? Don't you know that whoever you are, you're nothing but a junior employee and I am a minister and that no matter how far up the ladder you go, in the end you're a woman whose place is in bed underneath a man?'

What's that you say, Mother? Yes. Any woman hearing such words from any man would have died of shame, or would at least have fainted, especially if the man saying such things were not just any man but her superior in the government, who is not merely a manager or head of department, but a minister in person. And she didn't hear those words being said in an empty or closed room, but in my office, full of men, all of them senior employees. Yes, Mother, any woman in her place would surely have died of shame. I wanted to kill her by any means, even by shame. But the strange thing was, Mother, that nothing could kill this woman. She wasn't overcome by shame, didn't even lower her eyes, didn't blink an eyelid. Perhaps, Mother, you can imagine how much anger any man in my place, in my position, of my status and manliness and pride in my own eyes and in those of the employees in my ministry, would feel? And also because, Mother, I had never in all my life seen an employee raise his eyes to those of his superior, certainly never a woman raise hers to those of a man, not to her brother or father or superior, not even to her son. And what if that man were more important than her father or superior or any other man in his own and other people's opinion and in his self-respect and in people's respect for him?

Each time I remembered, Mother, how much respect I had for my masculinity and the respect people had for my position, my anger grew more intense. How could this woman do what she did? My anger, Mother, may have cooled a bit if I'd seen her blink, just once, or if her eyelids had trembled for just one second. But, Mother, she stood before me, her eyes raised to mine, as though I were not her boss and she not my subordinate, as though I were not a minister and she not a junior employee, as though I were not a man and she not a woman, as though I were not myself and she not herself. My anger grew each time I felt that I wasn't myself, that she wasn't herself. I asked myself who she was to make me feel that I was not myself. Or perhaps it was that I got more angry each time I remembered that I was indeed myself, with all the status, authority, masculinity and self-respect that is mine. I was absolutely sure, Mother, that I was myself, with all that meant. But, Mother, and this is what drove me crazy, at the same time I felt equally sure that I was not myself, that I would never be the same again. Maybe, Mother, you can appreciate my situation and can forgive me for hating this woman so much that the following day my temperature rose to 40°c and I had to stay at home, with my head burning under an ice-pack. And, Mother, my temperature did not go down until after I'd issued all the ministerial decisions in my power to break that woman and utterly destroy her.

What's that? No, not at all, Mother. I wasn't able to destroy her. She remained in existence, that woman. I happened to overhear some people say that she still existed. I didn't exactly overhear it, for I used to snoop around for information about her, fearful that someone would notice me, hoping to hear bad news or that she'd been destroyed in an accident. But no, Mother, that woman remained in existence. Not only did she remain as alive as any other woman but, Mother, I happened to see her once and she hadn't changed in the slightest. Her eyes were still raised and her eyelids did not tremble, even though, Mother, for all that, she was a woman like any other. I wasn't angry because she was a woman and I had never seen a woman do what she did. I wasn't angry because she was an employee and I had never seen an employee do what she did. No, what angered me and made me crazy was that I was incapable of destroying her by any decision or any authority and that she remained in existence. Her existence drove me mad, made me lose my dignity, my mind. I wanted to retrieve myself and my composure. But, Mother, she remained in existence and her existence began to threaten my own.

What's that? Yes, Mother. I don't know how I got into such a state. How could a junior employee, in the fifth or sixth grade, threaten the existence of any great man such as myself in a ministerial position. But I was really angry, more angry than I'd ever been in my life. I wasn't angry because I couldn't destroy her, with all the power at my disposal, nor because she did something no one else had done. No, what really angered me, Mother, was that she had done something I myself had never done. I have never, in all my life, been able to raise my eyes to those of any one of my superiors, even if he were a junior employee with only slight power over me. My anger grew, Mother, each time I tried to understand why I was incapable of doing that while she could, even though I'm a man and she's a woman, just like any other woman!

What's that? Yes, Mother. She was like any other woman. Like you, Mother, yes, like you. But I've never seen you, Mother, raise your eyes to anyone the way that woman did to me. Maybe if I'd seen you do it just once, I'd have been able to stand that employee. If you'd raised your eyes once to Father's, maybe I too would have been able to raise my eyes to his. Maybe I'd have been able to raise my eyes to those of any man in a position of authority. But, Mother, I've never seen you do it. If you'd done it only once, it may have been possible for me to do it too, because I did everything like you. Because, Mother, you were my sole example when I was a child and I used to imitate you, to imitate your every movement. I learned how to speak by moving my lips as you moved yours. I learned to walk by moving my legs as you moved your legs. I learned everything from you, Mother. So why didn't you raise your eyes to Father's so that I could have learned how to do it? Maybe if you'd done it just once, I'd have been able, as a child, to overcome my fear of him just once. And maybe, as an employee, I'd have been able to overcome my fear of any person in a position of authority.

What's that, Mother? No, my dear. I'm not blaming you. All I ask is that you stroke my head and neck and chest with your tender hand as you used to when I was a child, for you're the only one to whom I can open my heart, and to whom I can reveal my real tragedy. And the real tragedy is not that I lost my position as minister, but *how* I lost it. Perhaps the tragedy would have been somewhat lessened if I'd lost it for a serious or important or even plausible reason. The tragedy, Mother, is that the reason was not plausible and nobody can understand or believe it. Perhaps I did not know, Mother, that the reason was implausible until the day I opened the morning paper and did not find my name included amongst those of the new ministry. I suddenly felt absolutely sunk, as if my very name had fallen from my

20

body. Every day, as I searched the papers for my name and did not find it, my feeling that I'd become a nameless body was confirmed. The telephone, Mother, which used to ring each day and at each moment, calling my name, fell silent, deaf, inarticulate, as if it too were bringing me down, bringing down my name. Such a bitter feeling of downfall, Mother, I've never experienced in all my life.

What's that, Mother? Yes, my dear, I didn't know the taste of that which I'd lost until that moment. And I fear, Mother, that that's the way of all life. We don't know the taste until after we've lost it. That in itself, Mother, is a catastrophe, because time passes and the opportunity may be lost for ever. That was how it was as I sat by the silent telephone, waiting, scared that one of my family would notice me sitting and waiting. Then I'd act as if I wasn't waiting, even though I was. If only the phone had rung, just once, in any way, made any sound, man or woman, relative or stranger, big or small, human or animal, any voice, even the braying of a donkey. If only the phone had rung, just one time, and called my name.

What's that, Mother? No, my dear. The catastrophe was not that the telephone did not ring, nor that I wanted it to ring. The tragedy, Mother, was that I discovered that the ringing of the telephone, which I'd always said I hated, I didn't hate at all, but loved. The sound of the bell used to send a quiver of delight through my body which, had I only known it at the time, no power on earth could have taken from me. That delight,

21

Mother, was greater than the delight of sex and the delight of love and the delight of food and of everything in the world. It was an unearthly, inhuman delight, unknown to human instincts, an instinct without feeling and non-instinctual, an instinct which annihilated feeling, annihilated instincts. It alone remained strong, gigantic, tremendous, capable of annihilating anything in the world, wiping out tiredness, the pressure of work, wiping out dignity, insults, making my body capable of movement and activity even as I slept, making my mind work even in my dreams, making me stand on my feet in the airport under the rays of the sun after non-stop effort, features relaxed to welcome some official guest, making me sit with back and neck tensed up at some meeting or some reception, making me ready, at any moment of the day or night, to adopt the official position of legs pressed together and hands clasped over the chest or stomach. Yes, Mother. This gigantic delight was capable of wiping out any tiredness or effort, was even capable of wiping itself out, and myself with it, if it so desired.

What's that, Mother? Yes, my dear. I lost all this delight for the sake of some insignificant thing. And what is not insignificant compared to such delight? But, to tell the truth, Mother, that thing was not insignificant. It was not something simple, ordinary. No, it was not simple and not ordinary. It was the most serious thing that ever happened to me, the most serious thing I could ever face. Like death, Mother. Sometimes I used to believe I could face even death itself. But at the time I did not know what was happening to me. I sat in my chair as usual, alert in mind and body, my nerves and senses awake. My mind and body had turned into that nervous radar mass, naked and sensitive to any gesture or movement. I sat in my chair as normal, certain that I was normal, whilst with equal certainty, I knew that I was not normal and that, despite the fact that I was extremely alert, I was incapable of being alert and that, for the first time in my life, I was incapable of focusing my mind or of controlling it. My mind had begun to think by itself without me and was preoccupied with something with which I did not want to be preoccupied. That in itself would be a catastrophe if it happened to any employee in a meeting. So what about me, a minister, in this only meeting of importance, in which I was turned into a subordinate? The catastrophe, Mother, was not that my mind was out of my control, for had it been so in order to think of something important, like the annual report which I was to present or the new budget for which I was to ask, then maybe I'd have felt a little relaxed and comforted. But the catastrophe was that my mind did not think of anything important, but of something insignificant, the most insignificant thing that the mind of a man in a position such as mine, and particularly at such a meeting, could be occupied with.

What's that you say, Mother? No, my dear. I wasn't thinking about anyone. I was thinking about myself. I wanted to work out how to sit in my chair as normal, despite the fact that I wasn't normal. I wanted to work out whether it was me sitting in my chair or some other person and which of them was me. The problem, Mother, was not that I couldn't work it out, but rather that I knew that the reason for this catastrophe was none other than that junior employee. I curse the day I set eyes on her, for since then my mind has not stopped thinking about her. Perhaps I'd have found a little peace or comfort if what engrossed me was that she was a woman or a female. After all, I am a man and any man, no matter what his position, can still sometimes be engrossed in a woman. But the tragedy, Mother, was that at the time she didn't preoccupy me as a woman or a female because, in my view, she wasn't female at all. She was perhaps the only woman I've ever met in my life whom I did not feel for a second was a female. But what occupied and dominated my mind to the extent of stripping me of my willpower was that, although she was a female and although she was a junior employee, the most junior official who could enter a minister's office, she had managed to do something out of the ordinary, breaking every convention with which we are brought up from the time we're born, all the values we have known since the time we found ourselves alive and became human. The tragedy, Mother, was not that she did that and not that she did what no one else had done or what I myself had not done, but that from the time she'd done it, I was no longer myself. Whoever it was sitting in my chair was not me, but another person whom I hardly knew. I didn't even know which of the two was me. That, Mother, was the precise question which dominated my mind and body and all my senses at that meeting.

I tried so hard, Mother, to fight it. I mustered all my strength to resist it, to drive it from my mind, so that my left hand moved of its own accord as though to drive it out of my head. My right hand was, as usual, holding a pen over a piece of paper, poised and ready for any sign or sound. My left hand should have remained lying in my lap as normal, but it did not lie there. Whoever saw it move the way it did must have thought I was brushing away an obstinate fly from my face, but since the meeting hall was clean and completely free of flies, the cleanest hall in the whole country and the last hall on earth that a fly could enter, the movement of my left hand must have appeared abnormal. And since it was abnormal, it began to attract attention. I used to hate, Mother, to draw attention to myself at such important meetings, and always preferred to remain sitting in my chair completely unobtrusive or unnoticed until the meeting was over and I had not had to face any questions.

What's that, Mother? No, my dear. I wasn't frightened of questions and I wasn't afraid of not knowing the right answer, since the right answer was common knowledge and easy, easier than any other answer, easier that any maths problem I had to solve as a pupil, as easy as the simplest step in a multiplication table, two times two equals four. The difficulty, Mother, was that I wasn't scared of *not* giving the right answer but of *giving* the right answer.

What's that, my dear? Yes, Mother. That was the real catastrophe that happened that day. I don't know how it happened and I don't know if it was me who said it or the other person occupying my chair. I was still sitting in my chair, like I told you, and it seems that the repeated movement of my left hand had attracted attention because suddenly, he turned his eyes towards me, reminding me in a flash of my father's eyes when I was a child. As his eyes turned towards me, I tried to shrink back slightly or to move forward, just as I used to do as a pupil sitting in class, and hoped that his eyes would fall on the one sitting in front of me or behind me, and not on me. But that day I didn't move in my chair. Maybe I didn't notice the movement of his eyes at the right time, before they turned in my direction. Or perhaps I wasn't in full possession of my faculties at that moment. Or perhaps I was sick with fever and my temperature had risen. Or perhaps there was some other reason. The important thing, Mother, was that I didn't move in my chair and the full weight of his eyes fell on me, like the fall of death. When he asked me the question, my mouth opened of its own accord, involuntarily, as if it were the mouth of another person, an unthinking person quick to answer without much thought or great effort. And since it was an answer without much thought or great effort, it was the easy answer, the easiest and simplest of answers. It was, Mother, the obvious answer.

What's that, my dear? No, Mother. The obvious answer was not the right answer. The right answer is not the required answer. That, Mother, is the ABC of politics, as I told you at the start. It's the first lesson we learn in politics. How did I come to forget it, Mother? I don't know. But I did forget it at that moment. How it grieved me, Mother, to forget it. And my grief was so very, very strong that all feelings of grief disappeared, so much so that my feelings of relief were almost akin to joy. I felt, Mother, that a heavy burden had been lying on my chest and stomach, heavier than my two paralysed hands clasped over my chest and stomach, heavier even than my body sitting paralysed in my chair, heavier even than the chair and the earth beneath it, as if the earth itself were weighing on me.

What's that, Mother? Yes, my dear. I relaxed and what relaxation! How I feel this relaxation in these final moments as I leave the world and everything in it. But the catastophe, Mother, is that despite this relaxation and although I'm leaving this world, I still put the telephone beside my head and I'm still waiting for it to ring, just once. To hear the bell, just once. To hear a voice, any voice, say in my ear: 'Your Excellency, the Minister,' How I'd love to hear it, Mother, one time, only one time before I die.

The Veil

The Veil

All of a sudden I awake to find myself sitting, a bottle of wine in front of me of which only a little remains, and an ashtray full of cigarette ends of a strange kind I think I have not seen before, until I remember that they are the new brand I began smoking three or four years ago.

I look up from the ashtray to see a man I've never seen before. He is naked, apart from a silken robe which is open to reveal hairy chest and thighs. Between the chest and thighs are a pair of close-fitting striped underpants. I raise my surprised eyes to his face. Only now do I realize that I've seen him before. My eyes rest on his for a moment and I smile a strange, automatic smile, as fleeting as a flash of light or an electric current, leaving behind no trace other than a curious kind of perplexity like the eternal confusion of a person in search of God or happiness. Why is there such confusion in the world and in my body at this particular moment, even though each day my eyes meet hundreds or thousands of eyes and the world and my body remain as they are? But it is soon over. The world and my body return to normal and life continues as usual. It is three or four years since I saw him for the first time and I'd almost forgotten him in the tumult of work and home and people.

My eyes fall on to his naked body and hairy thighs once more. The expression on my face, as I look at his body, is not the same as when I look into his eyes, for my problem is that what I feel inside shows instantly on my face. His eyes are the only part of his body with which I have real contact. They dispel strangeness and ugliness and make my relationship with him real in the midst of numerous unreal ones. Three years, maybe four, and every time I run into him in a street or office or corridor, I stop for a moment in surprise and confusion. Then I continue on my way, knowing that whilst this relationship is very strange, it is at the same time familiar and accepted, among numerous unfamiliar and un-accepted relationships.

When we began meeting regularly or semi-regularly, my relationship with him did not extend to parts of his body other than his eyes. For long hours we would sit and talk, my eyes never leaving his. It was a sort of meeting of minds, and gratifying, but the gratification was somehow lacking. What did it lack?

I asked myself whether it was the body's desire for contact with another body? And why not? In the final analysis, isn't he a man and I a woman? The idea strikes me as new, even strange, and a frightening curiosity takes hold of me. I wonder what the meeting of my body with his could be like. A violent desire to find out can sometimes be more violent than the desire for love and can, at times, draw me into loveless contacts simply in order to satisfy that curiosity. And every time that happens, I experience a repulsion, certain in my mind that my body repulses the body of a man except in one situation – that of love.

I understand the cause of this repulsion. It's an explicable repulsion linked not to the body but to history. To the extent that man worships his masculinity, so woman repulses him. A woman's repulsion is the other face of the worship of the male deity. No power on earth can rid woman of her repulsion other than the victory of love over the male deity. Then history will go back six thousand years to when the deity was female. Will love be victorious? Is the relationship between us love? I do not know. I have no proof. Can love be proved? Is it the desire which rises to the surface of my crowded life, to look into his eyes? Like a person who, from time to time, goes to a holy water spring to kneel down and pray and then goes home? I do not kneel down and neither do I pray. I recognize no deity other than my mind inside my head. What is it that draws me to his eyes?

Is love simply a fairy tale, like the stories of Adam and Eve or Cinderella or Hassan the Wise? All the fairy tales came to an end and the veil fell from each of them. Many veils fell from my mind as I grew up. Each time a veil fell, I would cry at night in sadness for the beautiful illusion which was lost. But in the morning, I'd see my eyes shining, washed by tears as the dew washes the blossom, the jasmine and the rose. I would leave the mirror, trample the fallen veil underfoot and stamp on it with a new-found strength, with more strength than I'd had the previous day.

He has filled the tenth or twentieth glass. My hand trembles a little as I hold it, but the deity inside my head is as steady and immobile as the Sphinx. My eyes are still on his and do not leave them, even though I realize, somehow, that he is no longer wearing the silken robe nor even the tight striped underpants.

I notice that his body is white, blushed with red, revealing strength, youthfulness, cleanliness and good eating. My eyes must still have been staring into his, for in another moment, I realize that he has taken my head in his hand and moved it so that my eyes fall on to his body.

I look at him steadily and once again see the strength and youthfulness and cleanliness and good eating. I almost tell him what it is I see.

But I look up and my eyes meet his. I do not know whether it is he who looks surprised or whether the surprise is in my own eyes. I tell myself that the situation calls for surprise, for it is nearly three in the morning. The glass is empty. There is no one in the house and the world outside is silent, dark, dead, fallen into oblivion. What is happening between my body and his?

When I next turn towards him, he is sitting,

dressed in the robe with the belt carefully tied around his waist, hiding his chest and thighs. I no longer see anything of him other than his head and eyes and feet inside a pair of light house-shoes. From the side, his face looks tired, as though he's suddenly grown old and weary. His features hang loose, like a child needing to sleep after staying up late. I put out my hand, like a mother does to stroke the face of a child, and place a tender motherly kiss on his forehead.

In the street I lift my burning face to the cold and humid dawn breeze. Mysterious feelings of joy mingle with strange feelings of sadness. I put my head on my pillow, my eyes open, filled with tears. My mind had got the better of the wine until I put my head on the pillow; but then the wine took over and sadness replaced joy.

When I open my eyes the following day, the effect of the wine has gone and the veil has lifted from my eyes. I look in the mirror at my shining eyes washed with tears. I am about to walk away from the mirror, like every other time, to trample on the fallen veil at my feet and stamp on it with new-found strength. But this time I do not leave my place. I bend down, pick up the veil from the ground and replace it once again on my face.

The Greatest Crime

The Greatest Crime

I swear to you, whoever reads my story, that I was more innocent than you imagine, more innocent, perhaps, than many of you. I became certain of my innocence after I died (I am dead now and so I can express myself without fear of you). I was as innocent as a young child – which means (if you have a good memory) that I was not innocent at all, at least not in your view. And yet I did and still do consider myself as innocent as a young child. Not one of you remembers what went on in your head when you were a child and I too was like you when I was on earth. We forget our childhood when we grow up and we forget our dreams when we awake from sleep. Such forgetfulness is sure proof that in our childhood we did things that embarrass us when we are adults and that in our dreams we did things that embarrass us when we awake.

But I am no longer like you. The experience of death has given me an inhuman courage and I no longer need to section off the phases of my life nor to erect a thick wall to separate one from the other. I was able to acquire such a view of the disjointed and fragmented phases of your lives only after I left the earth. The spectacle of your lives before my eyes surprised me. It is really a very strange spectacle, resembling, to a large extent, the body of a person from which the head is cut and the legs amputated, and of which only the torso remains. It is also a frightening spectacle, reminding me of a train accident I witnessed as a young child. To this day I have not forgotten the sight of the body which had been taken out from under the wheels, without a head and without legs.

I have never forgotten that spectacle. Although, in fact, I did forget it. It is, perhaps, almost the only spectacle in my life which I did completely forget. It was so ugly that I totally forgot it. And it was so ugly that it remains in my memory and I have never forgotten it. That is what happens to you too; you forget and do not forget. And that's the cause of your suffering on earth.

But in any case, I no longer fear this spectacle and have acquired a strange courage. I can stare at it for a whole second. My courage has grown so much that I can even look into my father's face for a whole minute. My father's face was like the face of all fathers. And the faces of all fathers appear to me now like those cardboard masks which we used to buy on holidays. The eyes were not eyes but two large holes.

When I looked into them, I saw nothing. The nose was a protruding piece of cardboard and had two openings which were nothing but holes. Beneath the nose was a long black moustache and it was this moustache which used to make us laugh a lot when we were children. Each of us would take turns at wearing this mask which we'd bought for a penny and we'd try to frighten each other with that long black moustache.

I used to think that the reason I didn't love my father was because of his prickly black moustache. But now, when I stare at his face for the first time, I realize that I didn't love him because of his eyes. When I looked into his eyes, I understood immediately that it was he who killed my mother. When I was a child, I loved my mother. You do not understand what it means for a child to love its mother either, because you were never children (forgetfulness can make something that happened seem as though it had never happened). I loved my mother so much that I am incapable of describing her now, just as I was always incapable of describing her in the past. I used to imagine that I would be able to describe her once I was no longer on earth, now that everything earthly is over. But my love for my mother is not over. Only the unreal things are over while real things never end. My love for my mother was so real that I used to think that my mother was me. This was not just a belief but a feeling verging on certainty. Her body and mine were one. That bonding between myself and my mother still remains as it was when I was a child, for real things stay with us. Wherever we may be, whether we rise or fall in life, they remain as attached to us as

41

our own bodies. And my love for my mother was as real as my own body. I was a small child – and everything appears unreal in the eyes of a small child, as if in a dream. People are like ghosts or angels, a train runs on phantom rails and its whistle has a ring of magic, the sea is bottomless, the sky limitless, the street endless and the dark night as frightening as death.

I used to be frightened of two things: darkness and death. I'd slip out of my small bed in the middle of the night and creep into my mother's bed. I'd bury myself into her warm body and cling to her as hard as I could. I'd curl up to make my body smaller and try to shrink to the size of a foetus which could return to its mother's womb. My whole body shook with this fervent desire and trembled as in fever. I thought nothing could save me from imminent death in the darkness other than disappearing inside that warm and tender womb which would enclose me alone.

Anyone seeing me at that moment, curled up like a foetus, would have understood that this desire was real and that it was violent, that it was not so much a desire to escape death but rather to get close to my mother, so close as to stick to her, to merge my body in hers so that she and I could become one. I loved her so much that the obliteration of my body in hers was not obliteration, was not death, was not painful, was not frightening, but was the peak of my life, the climax of my pleasure, was security and total comfort.

In that state, I was not aware of anything. Everything around me had grown as warm as my mother's breasts and as silent as the inside of a womb. The world and everything in it – sea, sky, houses, trees, trains and rails – all vanished. All noise disappeared.

42

I no longer had ears or eyes or lips but only the senses of an unborn baby, feeling nothing but warmth, smelling nothing but milk.

In such a state, I was oblivious of the presence of my father who lay beside my mother with his huge body, his long black moustache trembling with the movement of his upper lip, his lower lip drooping under the pressure of a loud snore, a long thread of white spittle drooling slowly from the corner of his mouth and over his chin. Despite his deep sleep, from which it appeared to me at the time he would never awake, he opened his eyes. And although I could not see him (because I was curled up like a foetus), I noticed the look which flashed across his eyes and immediately vanished. At that time, I didn't know whether it had disappeared of its own accord or whether he had made it disappear, but I now know that it was he who did it. Despite the dark which immersed the bedroom and although I was unable to raise my eyes to his, that look was powerful enough to penetrate my skull like an arrow. Despite the pain of that penetration, despite the fear of it, despite the pitch-dark, and although it disappeared in a flash and there returned to his eyes the look of a loving father, despite all that, I knew the form of that look. It was the look of a man expressing hatred.

My father was a civilized man and like all civilized men of our time, who can control and hide their real feelings and display other feelings to show how they've progressed, like all of them, my father was able to hide his real desire to grasp my neck with his large fat fingers and fling me far away. His hand did in fact move towards me, but he resisted the movement so that it moved like the hand of a civilized father, patting his son on the shoulder. With a slow, quiet movement, he separated my body from the body of my mother and I found myself on the cold edge of the bed whilst he occupied my warm place.

It was wintertime and the night was cold. The woollen blanket reached only to the edge of the bed so that it covered just half my body and my back stayed bare. Then my father moved in his sleep and pulled the blanket towards himself so that I was completely uncovered. I shivered from the cold and my mother opened her eyes. In fact, I had not yet shivered, but she opened her eyes at the slightest movement. It may only have been the movement of the cover sliding off my back or a small muscle in my body contracting because of the cold. The movement may have happened or may have been about to happen. Even before the muscle contracted, she would suddenly open her eyes from the deepest sleep. Even before she opened her eyes, even before she awoke completely, she would reach out and cover me.

I used to be amazed and wonder at that secret, the secret of that strange telepathic power of her sleeping body to respond to the feelings of my body, despite the great distance between us which was occupied by the vast body of my father. My amazement grew when I heard my father accuse her of being a heavy sleeper. Once I heard him arguing with her because he had been ringing the bell for a long time before she awoke and opened the door. My father also accused her of not hearing well. Once he hit her (when she was feeding me on her lap) because he had been calling her to bring him his supper and she had not heard. Once I heard him tell her that her heart was cold and unfeeling. That day I saw my mother crying alone in the kitchen and timidly I went up to her and with half-formed words (I hadn't yet perfected the art of speech) I whispered in her ear, 'You have more feelings than Daddy, Mama.' Her eyes widened as she looked at me, surprised that such a small child could understand such a large truth. She enfolded me in her arms whispering, 'My darling.'

My father was standing at the door of the kitchen and saw me in her arms. That same fleeting look passed across his eyes. It appeared and immediately disappeared, penetrating my skull and making me quake violently with the sort of trembling that afflicts the body of a person face to face with death.

If he had done what a natural person does when he hates, if he had grabbed my neck with his large fingers, I would have relaxed and would have understood that he was behaving naturally towards me. Natural behaviour, however harsh, is always relaxing and reassuring. But my father was never reassuring. I was frightened of him, frightened of any movement he made. A quiet or gentle movement terrified me more than a violent or harsh movement. And whenever I was near him and saw his hand move, even if he was not going to do anything other than pat my shoulder or brush a fly from his face or scratch his ear, it made me jump and a concealed shudder would run over my body.

I didn't know why I was unable to sit close to

my father so that there was no distance between us. There always had to be a distance. Under no circumstances could I get so close to my father as to touch him, unlike my mother. When she sat next to me I would cling to her. It was not a normal clinging, but an urgent and violent desire to eliminate the distance between us, so that my body and hers would become one.

No one other than myself knew of this desire. I used to hide it, just like I hid my real feelings. When I sat in class and the teacher told me to repeat after him the sentence, 'I love my father as I love my mother,' I repeated it without protest: 'I love my father as I love my mother.' When I learned to write, the teacher told me to write my name, so I wrote 'Samir'. He then told me to write my full name, so I wrote 'Samir Aziza'. The teacher looked at my exercise book angrily, crossed out the name 'Aziza' with his red pen and said, 'Write your father's name!' I was surprised and opened my mouth to protest, but the teacher was big and I was small, so I meekly wrote 'Samir Adam'. The following day, the teacher chose me to repeat after him, 'I love my father as I love my mother,' and then the whole class chanted, 'I love my father as I love my mother.' The teacher told us to write it five times in our exercise books. The next day we wrote it once more and repeated it aloud several times. For homework too we had to write it five times and repeat it to ourselves ten times, then twenty times, until I found myself repeating it in my sleep: 'I love my father as I love my mother . . . I love my father as I love my mother . . .'

Once, my father heard me repeating it. And he smiled. His smile was strange. The structure of his face was not made for smiling. His forehead was prominent and wide and permanently fixed in a natural frown which did not disappear even when he slept. The bones of his face were thickset, the jaws as large and wide as those of a camel or horse. He could not disguise those jawbones, however much his lips separated to express a smile. I shuddered, the way I always did whenever I saw something unnatural. I had never seen a camel or a horse smile. 'Why don't horses or camels smile?' I asked my teacher at school. He replied, 'Only human beings can smile, Samir.'

My father did not know what was going on in my head. Some strange power enabled me to hide my real feelings. I raised my voice when I read the lesson from my exercise book: 'I love my father as I love my mother . . . I love my father as I love my mother . . .' I knew that I was lying, and because I knew that I was lying I was frightened that my father would find out. In order to deceive my father, I began to raise my voice louder and repeated, 'I love my father as I love my mother.' Each time I raised my voice, my fear grew that the lie would show. So I raised my voice more and more to hide the lie, and each time I did so, the lie showed more and each time my fear grew. It went on like that until I found myself screaming like someone crying out for help: 'I love my father as I love my mother! . . . I love my father as I love my mother! . . .'

My father never discovered the truth. When he saw the tears running down my cheeks, he approached me. But, as usual, I stepped back. As he came nearer, I took another step back. He came nearer. I stepped back. He raised his hand a little. I think that he was going to pat me on the shoulder, but it seemed to me then that his hand would fall on my face with a heavy slap. I jumped back to protect myself. My father stopped for a moment, his eyes wide in surprise, looking and staring at me, as if wondering what the reason was. It was not the natural wonderment of a person who is ignorant of the reason. It was unnatural, the reason known, and not only known but positively tangible and felt by all the feelings and senses of the body.

At such moments, a person becomes nervous. A person is not by nature inclined to such definite feelings but rather to doubt. However, nothing is as unbearable in life as doubt and that's the cause of your suffering on earth, for you live in both certainty and doubt.

But at that time I was a small child and was not able to rid him of either doubt or certainty. I had done everything in my power to memorize my lesson and repeat it aloud and had done everything in my power to make my voice sound real when I read it.

And my voice really did sound real. I couldn't do more than I had done. But my father remained standing before me. I did not see him because my head was bowed and my eyes were on the ground. I never dared to lift my head and look into his eyes. I knew that the moment my eyes met his, he would find out the fearful truth. And the fearful truth was that doubt would become certainty or that certainty would become doubt. But although my head was bowed, I could feel that look penetrating my head, piercing through it and pressing my back against the wall.

And so I stayed, standing before him, unable to retreat backwards, separated from him by only one step. I knew that in a moment the distance between us would disappear and that I would become one with the wall. I pressed my back to the wall with all my strength but the wall was as solid as rock.

At that moment my mother appeared, as though she'd suddenly materialized from out of the ground. I don't know how she appeared or from where, because that day she hadn't been at home but was spending the night at my aunt's. I don't know exactly what happened to me when I saw her. Of its own accord, my body leapt towards her, with urgency and violence, the urgency of escaping from death and the violence of clinging on to life. My body, at that time, acted naturally when it clung and stuck to her. It clung on so strongly that my body became one with hers.

When I think of that day, I tell myself that I wish I hadn't done what I did. I wish my back had stayed against that wall for ever. Or that I had become one with the wall. But I didn't know what was going to happen. The tragedy is that a person does not know what is going to happen the next day, let alone the next moment. This ignorance is like blindness and in fact really is blindness. I can see you now, walking before me without eyes. Your eyes are not eyes but holes through which the air passes, like the eyes of those cardboard masks I used to buy on holidays.

I still remember that day and have never forgotten it, like the spectacle of that headless and legless body which I have never forgotten. My memory has retained everything that happened that day, even though it is very far away and despite all the years that have passed, so many years that I cannot count them. I had only learned numbers up to ten, counting on my fingers, for the teacher had not yet taught us more than that. But despite the long years I still remember everything, no matter how insignificant, every movement, no matter how simple it seemed. But none of my father's movements were simple, however simple they appeared. I could pick up that rapid fleeting look in his eyes. I saw the black of his eyes fix on my mother. I was still in her arms, hiding my head against her chest. I no longer saw my father's face, but I felt my mother's arms around me, holding on to me with all her might, enclosing me in her body, folding around me and surrounding me, clasping me as though she wanted, were she able, to take me inside herself, even into the womb itself.

At that point, my father could no longer maintain his unreal face. With a rapid movement, he raised his hand and I saw his face with its large wide jaws like that of a wild hyena. For the first time, the face of my father before me became natural. I was no longer afraid as I had been earlier. I don't know how my courage returned, but I said to him, whispering at first, 'I don't love you.' As he momentarily froze before me, I picked up more courage and raised my voice louder and said to him, 'I don't love you.' When I heard my own voice clearly in my ears and was sure it was mine, I became increasingly courageous and said, 'I don't love you.' I continued like that until I found myself screaming in one long continuous and endless cry, 'I don't love you!'

He leapt at me like a rapacious tiger. But my mother was faster than he. In the twinkling of an eye, my mother's ample body was between him and me. I didn't see her face because I was standing behind her, but I knew from the way the muscles of her back were contracted and the way she was standing that she was like a tigress preparing to pounce. I don't know exactly what happened next. Voices stopped being human and everything changed in a moment. Even the seconds were no longer seconds, since time had changed and was no longer time. I was incapable of understanding anything around me, even myself and the reality of my existence, whether I was alive or dead. It seemed to me that I died and awoke, died and awoke, ten times, one hundred times, a thousand times, endlessly, as if my body had fallen into a bottomless abyss spinning terrifyingly fast, faster than the spin of the earth on its axis.

Suddenly the movement of the earth beneath my feet stopped and time stopped with it. Everything stopped and froze. I opened my eyes to see my mother's body on the ground. I thought that she was sleeping, as she usually slept on the ground in the summer. Timidly, I went up to her and whispered in her ear, 'Mama.' But she didn't answer. I was surprised, for she used to awaken at the slightest sound, would awaken even before a sound was made, before a word had come from my lips, would open her eyes and awake. Even before she opened her eyes, I would feel her body move. Before my lips moved, before I had said a word, before I myself heard it, she would have heard it.

Although I somehow realized that there was no way she could hear me, I kept whispering in her ear. When my father came with my uncles and carried her away from me and the house was without her, I was surprised. It was not the usual surprise which adults experience, but the surprise of a child, a strange surprise, when all things appear unreal, as though what had happened had not happened, a dream like reality, reality like a dream. My father moved to another house and took me with him. Days and years passed. I grew up, grew old and died. And yet I still imagined that what happened had not happened.

It is only now, after leaving the earth, that I am able to see the earth clearly. And I see you clearly too. Only now do I understand the greatest crime which has been committed in secret and which no one knows about. The first crime in the life of humanity was not that Cain slaughtered Abel but that Adam killed my mother. He killed her because I loved her and did not love him. And I wish he had realized that I could have loved him had he loved me. But my father was incapable of loving. Even though I was a child. I understood that he did not love me. And he did not love my mother. He loved only to satisfy himself.

Masculine Confession

Masculine Confession

Pour me another glass of wine, with a lot of ice. Let me talk and don't interrupt me. From time to time you can stroke my head or neck or chest or any part of my body you like, only don't stop me talking, because I came to you tonight to confess things I can't confess to anyone else, not even to God's agents on earth.

Actually, I don't believe in such agents and I dislike any intermediaries between myself and God. That doesn't mean that I'm proud or arrogant or that I deal haughtily with people. Quite the opposite. I'm humble and compassionate, and I am concerned for all people and for myself as one of them.

My self-concern is limitless, because I love myself. Yes, I confess to you that my only true love is my love of myself. I fell in love with myself the moment my mother gave birth to me. Her eyes shone as she said to my father: It's a boy! I loved my masculinity and from the start I realized it was the reason for my being privileged. I always had to prove its existence, declare it, show it to people to make it clear and visible and so firm that it was not open to doubt.

One day, when I was young, I was standing in the street beside my father, when suddenly a big fat foot trod on my toes. I screamed 'ow' in pain. My father looked at me angrily and said harshly: A man never says 'ow'. Since that day, I have never said 'ow'. I would hold back the pain and the tears when I was hurt or someone hit me and would brace the muscles of my back and neck and tell myself: I'm a man.

Once, when the doctor was digging his sharp scalpel into the sole of my foot to remove a splinter of glass, I felt my flesh tear and the blood flow. I was drowning in a sea of sweat from so much pain, but I didn't say 'ow'. That night, when everybody was asleep, I found myself crying in my sleep, softly murmuring 'ow, ow' until the morning.

When I awoke, I braced my back and neck muscles, put on my masculinity and wore it proudly, telling myself: I'm a man. What did you say, my dear? My feet and fingers are as soft as yours? That's true. I belong to the leisured class, the bourgeoisie, in other words. I only use my fingers to hold a glass of wine or to sign my name on some papers in the office or to wave to friends. My friends are many, as you know, and I love them all, just as I love all people. In other words, I love nobody. That doesn't mean that I hate them. It's just that I'm always self-concerned, always absorbed in loving myself. I'm ready at any time to defend myself, by any means, even by committing murder.

Don't look at me like that, as though I'm the only criminal on earth. Crime in the lives of us men is a matter of necessity. It's the only possible way for a man to prove he's a man. But since crime calls for bravery or authority, I'm unable to be a criminal. All I have are daydreams in which I imagine myself a bold hero, separating heads from bodies with a rapid blow of my sword. We men have great admiration for murderers. A man cannot admire another man without hating him. That's the reason I feel so ill at ease when I'm amongst important men in authority. And that's why I run away from the company of reputable men and why I feel at ease in the company of disreputable men. But in general, I prefer the company of women. For with a woman, no matter how important she is, one privilege remains mine – my masculinity. What did you say? Please don't interrupt me. Pour me another glass of wine, with a lot of ice, and let me unburden the crimes which weigh on my heart.

I'm not lying to you. All my crimes are human because they have one aim – to prove that I'm a man. No man can prove his masculinity except by beating other men. So I could not avoid entering into the eternal conflict, the conflict with all other men. In conference rooms or in bedrooms, the conflict is one and the same. Since in conference rooms I lack courage and authority, there's nothing left for me other than bedrooms. Don't call me a wolf or a womanizer. No, I'm a married man. I love my wife like I love my mother, with the same sort of spiritual, holy love. In other words, a love in which I take everything and to which I give nothing. That's ideal love. My wife is the only person (and before her it was my mother) with whom I can get angry and at whom I can rage freely. The reason's well known. She can't return my anger in the same way. We men can't show our anger with those who can be angry with us. I am never angry with my boss, but I get angry quickly with my mother. And with my wife I get angry and rage freely, as I do with my children. All of them I provide for and feed and if they got angry with me, they wouldn't find anyone to replace me.

That's what marriage is for. How else would it be possible for a man to give vent to his anger if it weren't for marriage? The poorest man from the lowest social class goes home to his wife, in the end, in order to be angry and to feel that he's a man. What did you say, my dear?

That's why you refused to get married? You're an intelligent woman. I don't think it's only your intelligence that draws me to your bed, you above all other women. So why is it to you especially that I confess, like a man does to his god? Why do I creep from my wife's bed every night to come to you? I'm not lying to you. It's not love, because as I said, I fell in love with myself from the start and that's the beginning and end of it.

The reason, my dear, is that you're the only person with whom I don't have to prove myself a man. That wasn't clear to me in the beginning. I used to ask myself: what ties me to this woman, why do I need her so much? I discovered the reason that night. Do you remember? It was the night I came to you after my shattering defeat to my rival in the election and the violent argument I had with my wife when I found her naked in my friend's arms. I came to you and cried in your arms and as I cried I felt as though the tears had been bottled up inside me, like steam under pressure, ever since the time my father told me off when I was a child and had said: A man never says 'ow'. That night I saw my tears flow like a river and heard my voice shout 'ow' over and over again. When I came to, I found my head at your feet, kneeling at your altar like a person kneels in a house of worship. What did you say, my dear? You saw the first real smile on my face? I told you it was the happiest night of my life? It's true. For the first time in my life, I discovered how stupid I'd been. When I was a boy, I almost lost an eye in a fight to prove myself a man. In my teens, I nearly lost my life on a number of occasions because of my perpetual readiness to compete. As an adult, I almost lost my mental faculties because of my defeat and then my wife's betrayal. But everything changed that night. The false mask which we call masculinity fell away and I began to see my real self. For the first time, I discovered that I did not have to prove to myself or to others that I was a man. What does 'man' mean, after all? This discovery was the happiest moment in my life. I was so happy, I began to smother you with kisses, to kiss your feet and rub my nose in them and cry. I found that the taste of my tears and my lowly position at your feet was sweet. What did you say? I confessed my love to you that night? Yes, my dear, I told you that I loved you. But I admit that as soon as I left your place and went back home and then to my office, I felt ashamed of myself. I was ashamed when I realized how I'd revealed to you a hidden part of myself, the feminine part, the part which all men hide as an imperfection. I was so ashamed that I decided never to see you again. But I returned to you the following night and the next night and every night, without a break. I know that I am bound to you by the force of my desire not to be a man but to be myself, as I am. But I'm also bound to this false masculine world. I put on the mask and take my place in the ranks. I play my part. I deliver blows whenever the other cannot hit me and I receive blows from those above me without responding. I suppress my anger until I get home to my wife and I hold back the tears until I come to you. It's a fair division, my dear. Men like us need at least two women. A woman with whom he can get angry and a woman with whom he can cry. What did you say, my dear? Yes, my wife loves me. She betrayed me because she loves me so much. I wasn't sure of that, but now I'm convinced of it. I am devoted to my wife and desire her more and more. Yes, I desire her more, my dear, because through her I have discovered something new that I couldn't have discovered by myself. I discovered that I'm not the only man on earth. I confess to you that I feel very comforted by this discovery. It's the comfort of surrendering to a fact to which I was unable to surrender before. If men experienced such comfort just once, they'd encourage their wives to betray them as quickly as possible. How many years I lost without this comfort, my dear.

What did you say? I'm very late? Yes, yes. But I'm luckier than others. Some men die believing they're the only one on earth.

What did you say? Women know this from the start? Yes, my dear. Women are smarter than men. A woman always knows that she's not the only woman on earth. Pour me another glass, with a lot of ice. Let me die in your arms and don't interrupt me.

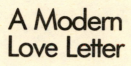

A Modern
Love Letter

A Modern
Love Letter

I am writing this letter to you, my friend, so that you may perhaps understand me or that I may perhaps understand myself. The attempt may come to nothing, for who is able to understand himself or the other? Who is able to break the shell? Just as attempting to break it merely confirms that it is not broken, so attempting to understand only increases the feeling of not understanding. And yet I try. I realize for certain that the attempt is futile but that does not stop me trying, just as I do not give up living my life, knowing that death is inevitable.

You may or may not be surprised that I call this a love letter, since in our relationship we have never mentioned the word love. We may have used other words, like affection or friendship or esteem. But these words are meaningless, imprecise. What is the meaning of the word 'affection' which we once used to describe our relationship? It doesn't mean a thing. It means neither love nor lack of love, but is a halfway feeling between love and no love, a halfway position between something and nothing, when a person loves and doesn't love, is angry and is not angry, hates and doesn't hate, speaks and doesn't speak, and always holds the rope in the centre. It is that fluid moderate position in everything which psychologists praise and to which they give the name mental health. Such health, in their view, consists of moderation in all things – in intelligence, in enthusiasm, in love, in hate, in ambition, in honesty.

And because honesty knows no moderation, so a person must lie to a certain extent to win the stamp of mental health from psychologists. And since love, like honesty, knows no moderation, so the word 'affection' means nothing in a relationship.

What is the relationship between us? How did it develop? Did it have a starting point? Did it, in other words, begin at the first meeting or at the last meeting or in the middle? I try now to gather the threads of my memory, to recall when the first meeting was, how your features appeared to me. The attempt seems to me now to be impossible, like trying to remember the first time I saw my face in the mirror. Or my mother's face. Or that of my father. There are some features which, the moment we set eyes on them, appear as though we have known them all along, as though they were part of us or within us and not external to us. Do you remember the first time you saw me? When was it? In your office? In my

66

office? In your house? In my house? In a field or at one of those gatherings where intellectuals always meet? Those faces tense when both smiling and frowning, cheeks distended both in speech and silence, stomach muscles slack when inhaling and exhaling, glances always fixed upwards, whatever that upwards is, red or green, valuable or cheap.

When I look into your eyes, I do not feel that you belong to this class. I see a different expression in your eyes which makes things different, less contradictory. Your smile is a smile, your frown a frown. Your features move with the muscles of your face in a spontaneous natural movement. I neither see it nor feel it and yet I know it exists, like the movement of time or of the earth or of an aeroplane which, although I do not feel it when I am inside it, I know to be there.

Sometimes that expression appears when I am sleeping or walking in the street or sitting or driving my car or engrossed in work. It remains before me, strangely compelling, taking me out of the state I was in, willing me to look at it, to understand the reason for its urgency. I push it away gently at first, then forcefully, then harshly, then with an anger resembling madness.

Once it pestered me with such insistence that I asked myself whether it was really a feeling of loneliness. My office is crowded, my house is crowded, Cairo is crowded. But, as in all such large cities, we live with crowdedness and loneliness at one and the same time. Between one person and another, despite close bodily contact, there is a thick wall which gets higher as people rise up the social ladder. And at night, when the city is immersed in sleep, I look around me like an orphan. I open my address book and flick through the names and telephone numbers, many numbers and many names, all set out in alphabetical order. And yet there is no one who can dispel the loneliness. This sprawling city stretched out before me is devoid of men. And yet it is crammed with males, not one of whom can meet a woman alone without thinking of jumping on her. Life in our world is made for men and nothing in it can amuse a woman other than that sort of amusement which neither amuses nor gratifies me and which only shows life in its ugliness and man in his baseness.

From time to time my phone rings and from time to time I accept some man's invitation out of my desire to find out the truth and to learn about life and people. It is also an attempt to dispel loneliness. I realize the impossibility of living inside myself, of remaining without others. If I wrote for myself alone, I would choke on my words. If I spoke to myself alone, my voice would fail. If I looked at my own face all the time, I would lose my mind.

And yet I always run from others. I love to disappear far away from them but I do so in order to remain in their thoughts. It is distance for the sake of closeness, separation for the sake of contact. And that's my dilemma. I want to be a separate entity and at the same time I want to be an inseparable part of others. This contradiction tears me apart, splitting me into two, one part inside myself far from others, the other part outside myself in the heart of others. One part is quiet and immobile and observes the movement of the other. Is it I who observes the other or is it the other which observes me? Which of us is motionless in time and place and which of us moves within time and on earth?

I am preoccupied with the answer to these questions, whilst the man who has invited me sits silently before me, looking at me now and again to catch some movement or a glance from me which could encourage him to invite me to bed. When he finds nothing, he is surprised. He may wonder if I am affected by twentieth-century complexes or if I am like a cave woman and still like rape and pain.

I cannot deny that the idea of rape, like the idea of suicide, holds some attraction for me and has been with me since time immemorial, no matter how I wrestle with its vestiges or seeds. But I do not commit suicide and nobody can rape me. No matter how difficult my life becomes, however much I suffocate, I do not commit suicide. However much a man desires me, he cannot overpower me. It is not, as you once told me, that I kill or castrate men, but I am always able to stare a man in the eyes and can always see the muscle around his mouth or his fingers quiver. It may only be quick and last no longer than a moment or two, but it is always enough for me to see it and to bend his will to mine. His muscular power, even the power of all the men in the world, is incapable of making the muscles of my hand yield under his.

You told me once that I was a strong woman. The truth is that I'm not always strong. Sometimes I let my hand yield. Sometimes I feel as lost as a tiny speck in the grip of a wild surge or in the grasp of some vast creature as predatory as fate and I feel unable to do anything of my own will or choice, incapable of holding on to truth and reality. You once asked me about my dreams. In truth, most of the time I live in my dreams for I can choose and change them, whereas it is reality which changes me without my choosing. I no longer see reality as real unless it is rooted in my dreams. I admit to you that my unconscious is stronger than my conscious mind and most of the time I obey it.

I saw you in one of my dreams. You were sitting with me somewhere far from the world, a place enclosing us alone, something that has never happened in reality. I was sitting beside you. Deep inside me there was a violent movement, stillness and quiet on the surface. I had a feeling of some sort of sad and mysterious happiness, a silent pulse in the body, an intense elation and a desire so strong it went beyond desire. I don't know what it was exactly that I wanted. That your eyes should remain on mine for ever? That you should raise your arms and encircle me and hide me inside yourself for ever? I awoke from sleep but you remained where you were beside me. I closed my eyes to rid myself of you, but you stayed, near to me, almost but not quite touching me, almost but not quite leaving me. Why? Why didn't you leave me? Is there something obligatory between us? Does anyone obligate you? Does anyone obligate me? I know there is no one, no one at all. And yet, I cannot say that I go to you from choice or will or that our relationship is not as vital to me as the air that enters and leaves my chest or the blood that flows in my veins.

This involuntary side of my relationship with you arouses rebellion in me, for I value my freedom. That's why I rebel against you. At times I tell you I won't see you again. Or I try to pile up your mistakes or slips of the tongue and may accuse you of things of

70

which I accuse other men. But it is always a failed revolution, at times resembling my revolution against myself, at times making me want to throw my body from the window and rid myself of it for ever. The result is always the same. My body remains attached to me and you remain in your place before my eyes, near to me, almost but not quite touching me. Why? Why do you never touch me? Are you simply a ghost? Do you exist in reality?

Sometimes, when you used to see me to the door, I would feel as though you briefly touched my hand or put your arm around my waist, a light rapid touch which no sooner happened than was gone. It may not even have been a touch since there was always a distance between your hand and my body, a hair's breadth, but always enough to separate us and for my moment of certainty to vanish. Again I ask myself whether it was real or a dream? Why does this distance always remain? Is it my fear of you? Is it your fear of me? Is there really anything to fear?

Once I wanted to dispel the dream, to reach out and touch certainty. I invited you to my house. Do you remember the date? In your voice I heard an unusual tremor of surprise or hesitation or fear or uncertainty. You did not come. I did not ask you why. I knew that, like me, you always want to waver between certainty and doubt.

Is there anything to dispel doubt? Is there proof of anything? There is nothing definite between me and you that I can cling to, no appropriate word, no language, no movement, no touch, nothing at all between us to confirm anything. But there is one thing of which I'm sure (and which also cannot be proved), and that is that you feel towards me what I

71

feel for you, to the same extent, in the same way and at the same time. Am I mistaken? I may or may not be.

That's how I am, my friend. I draw near to you and then draw back. I appear and disappear. I step forward and then I retreat. I decide on confrontation and then I run away. Day after day, month after month, twenty months or more. You once told me that our lives are passing, that a day that has gone will not return, that I'm wasting my life searching for the impossible or the absolute, that no one except God can satisfy me. One day I was hiding my eyes behind a pair of large sunglasses and you asked me to take them off, which I did. When you looked into my eyes, I nearly confessed to you that you are the only certainty and truth in my life. But the telephone or the doorbell rang or something happened or perhaps one of your children appeared or maybe you looked away or moved your head or arm. It seems to me that you glanced at the clock, deliberately or not. It lasted no longer than a second but it was enough to tear the fine silken hair on which was balanced the feeling of certainty.

You told me once that I run away from life, that I am incapable of loving, that I suffer from the sickness of the age, that I need pills or medicine or something of the sort. I was surprised and not surprised, sad for myself and not sad. I was on the verge of feeling ill and of swallowing the pills of the twentieth-century. You asked me more than once why I did not take pills, like all intellectuals. But, my friend, I do not belong to this age, neither am I one of those intellectuals. I don't read the newspapers as they do. My eyes close in spite of themselves when they look at the papers and my ears shut when they hear the news being read. When I walk in the street I do not see faces and I appear to people to be blind and deaf. But, my friend, I am neither blind nor deaf. I see every face that passes in front of me and I read every letter written on the face of the earth and I hear every sound, even the patter of an ant or the beat of an orphan heart in the breast of a child. Do you think I'm talking nonsense? Do you really think I don't see? I saw you once when I was walking along Tahrir Street. Your car was moving fast, like all the other cars. Your face was tired, like all the other faces and your eyes were sad, like all other eyes. It was very crowded, bodies crammed together, vehicles crammed together. The air was stagnant and sticky. Everyone was panting in a sea of sweat, practically suffocating, shouting for help, begging to be saved. But nobody saw anyone else. Nobody heard anyone else. Nobody saved anyone else.

Despite the speed of your car, I managed to study your face for a brief moment. Your features were not your features, your eyes not your eyes. I wondered whether it was you or not. I quickly turned around. Your car had almost vanished in the crowd but I managed to catch the number. I stood still for a moment, wondering where you had come from and where you were going and why you were going so fast. I knew that you were coming from your office and were on your way home or going to an appointment with someone big or small, someone sick or well. I knew all that and yet I stood looking around in surprise as though I knew nothing.

Then I continued on my way again, my head and heart heavy with a cold creeping depression and a question with no answer: Why all this? What's it all for? Is it the pursuit of money? Or the attempt to gain power? Or is it the search for fame? But you have a great deal of all these things. What is it then? Can it be love? But does love make a face tired and the eyes sad?

I felt I hated this city, those faces, those eyes, the hands of the clock, everything. The hatred was so intense that I tried to close my eyes and ears and all the pores of my body. I had a violent desire to run as fast as possible and get away from everything, a violent desire to separate myself from the world, to the point of dying.

But one thing I did not want – to lose your face in the crowd, that in time you should vanish from before my eyes. You know, my friend, that I don't want anything from you. I eat and drink and sleep and have sex and drive a car like yours. But I don't want to lose you in this crowd. Life without you is like a silent black-and-white movie. But with you, everything changes. Colours return and all things are luminous.

At this moment I wish that I could hold your hand in mine, that my whole life would become delicate tender fingers to touch your face, that my whole body would split into millions of tiny fingers to wipe the tiredness from your eyes. After all this, can you still accuse me of being incapable of loving? Can you again tell me that I don't understand, that I don't have natural intelligence? Can you now understand me a little? And do I understand you a little? I hope so. It must be so!

In Camera

In Camera

The first thing she felt was a blinding light. She saw nothing. The light was painful, even though her eyes were still shut. The cold air hit her face and bare neck, crept down to her chest and stomach and then fell lower to the weeping wound, where it turned into a sharp blow. She put one hand over her eyes to protect them from the light, whilst with the other she covered her neck, clenching her thighs against the sudden pain. Her lips too were clenched tight against a pain the like of which her body had never known, like the sting of a needle in her eyes and breasts and armpits and lower abdomen. From sleeping so long while standing and standing so long while sleeping, she no longer knew what position her body was in, whether vertical or horizontal, dangling in the air by her feet or standing on her head in water.

The moment they sat her down and she felt the seat on which she was sitting with the palms of her hands, the muscles of her face relaxed and resumed their human form. A shudder of sudden and intense pleasure shook her from inside when her body took up a sitting position on the wooden seat and her lips curled into a feeble smile as she said to herself: Now I know what pleasure it is to sit!

The light was still strong and her eyes still could not see, but her eyes were beginning to catch the sound of voices and murmurings. She lifted her hand off her eyes and gradually began to open them. Blurred human silhouettes moved before her on some elevated construction. She suddenly felt frightened, for human forms frightened her more than any others. Those long, rapid and agile bodies, legs inside trousers and feet inside shoes. Everything had been done in the dark with the utmost speed and agility. She could not cry or scream. Her tongue, her eyes, her mouth, her nose, all the parts of her body, were constrained. Her body was no longer hers but was like that of a small calf struck by the heels of boots. A rough stick entered between her thighs to tear at her insides. Then she was kicked into a dark corner where she remained curled up until the following day. By the third day, she still had not returned to normal but remained like a small animal incapable of uttering the simple words: My God! She said to herself: Do animals, like humans, know of the existence of something called God?

Her eyes began to make out bodies sitting on that elevated place, above each head a body, smooth

78

heads without hair, in the light as red as monkeys' rumps. They must all be males, for however old a woman grew, her head could never look like a monkey's rump. She strained to see more clearly. In the centre was a fat man wearing something like a black robe, his mouth open; in his hand something like a hammer. It reminded her of the village magician, when her eyes and those of all the other children had been mesmerized by the hand which turned a stick into a snake or into fire. The hammer squirmed in his hand like a viper and in her ears a sharp voice resounded: The Court! To herself she said: He must be the judge. It was the first time in her life she'd seen a judge or been inside a court. She'd heard the word 'court' for the first time as a child. She'd heard her aunt tell her mother: The judge did not believe me and told me to strip so he could see where I'd been beaten. I told him that I would not strip in front of a strange man, so he rejected my claim and ordered me to return to my husband. Her aunt had cried and at that time she had not understood why the judge had told her aunt to strip. I wonder if the judge will ask me to strip and what he will say when he sees that wound, she said to herself.

Gradually, her eyes were growing used to the light. She began to see the judge's face more clearly. His face was as red as his head, his eyes as round and bulging as a frog's, moving slowly here and there, his nose as curved as a hawk's beak, beneath it a yellow moustache as thick as a bundle of dry grass, which quivered above the opening of a mouth as taut as wire and permanently gaping like a mousetrap.

She did not understand why his mouth stayed open. Was he talking all the time or breathing through it? His shiny bald head moved continually with a nodding movement. It moved upwards a little and then backwards, entering into something pointed; then it moved downwards and forwards, so that his chin entered his neck opening. She could not yet see what was behind him, but when he raised his head and moved it backwards, she saw it enter something pointed which looked like the cap of a shoe. She focused her vision and saw that it really was a shoe, drawn on the wall above the judge's head. Above the shoe she saw taut legs inside a pair of trousers of expensive leather or leopard skin or snakeskin and a jacket, also taut, over a pair of shoulders. Above the shoulders appeared the face she'd seen thousands of times in the papers, eyes staring into space filled with more stupidity than simplicity, the nose as straight as though evened out by a hammer, the mouth pursed to betray that artificial sincerity which all rulers and kings master when they sit before a camera. Although his mouth was pinched in arrogance and sincerity, his cheeks were slack, beneath them a cynical and comical smile containing chronic corruption and childish petulance.

She had been a child in primary school the first time she saw a picture of the king. The face was fleshy, the eyes narrow, the lips thin and clenched in impudent arrogance. She recalled her father's voice saying: he was decadent and adulterous. But they were all the same. When they stood in front of a camera, they thought they were god.

Although she could still feel her body sitting on

the wooden seat, she began to have doubts. How could they allow her to sit all this time? Sitting like this was so very relaxing. She could sit, leaving her body in a sitting position, and enjoy that astounding ability which humans have. For the first time she understood that the human body differed from that of an animal in one important way – sitting. No animal could sit the way she could. If it did, what would it do with its four legs? She remembered a scene that had made her laugh as a child, of a calf which had tried to sit on its backside and had ended up on its back. Her lips curled in a futile attempt to open her mouth and say something or smile. But her mouth remained stuck, like a horizontal line splitting the lower part of her face into two. Could she open her mouth a little to spit? But her throat, her mouth, her neck, her chest, everything, was dry, all except for that gaping wound between her thighs.

She pressed her legs together tighter to close off the wound and the pain and to enjoy the pleasure of sitting on a seat. She could have stayed in that position for ever, or until she died, had she not suddenly heard a voice calling her name: Leila Al-Fargani.

Her numbed senses awoke and her ears pricked up to the sound of that strange name: Leila Al-Fargani. As though it wasn't her name. She hadn't heard it for ages. It was the name of a young woman named Leila, a young woman who had worn young woman's clothes, had seen the sun and walked on two feet like other human beings. She had been that woman a very long time ago, but since then she hadn't worn a young woman's clothes nor seen the sun nor walked on two feet. For a long time she'd been a small animal inside a dark and remote cave and when they addressed her, they only used animal names.

Her eyes were still trying to see clearly. The judge's head had grown clearer and moved more, but it was still either inside the cap of the shoe whenever he raised it or was inside his collar whenever he lowered it. The picture hanging behind him had also become clearer. The shiny pointed shoes, the suit as tight as a horseman's, the face held taut on the outside by artificial muscles full of composure and stupidity, on the inside depraved and contentious.

The power of her sight was no longer as it had been, but she could still see ugliness clearly. She saw the deformed face and remembered her father's words: They only reach the seat of power, my girl, when they are morally deformed and internally corrupt.

And what inner corruption! She had seen their real corruption for herself. She wished at that moment they would give her pen and paper so that she could draw that corruption. But would her fingers still be capable of holding a pen or of moving it across a piece of paper? Would she still have at least two fingers which could hold a pen? What could she do if they cut off one of those two fingers? Could she hold a pen with one finger? Could a person walk on one leg? It was one of those questions her father used to repeat. But she hated the questions of the impotent and said to herself: I will split the finger and press the pen into it, just as Isis split the leg of Osiris. She remembered that old story, still saw the split leg pouring with blood. What a long nightmare she was living! How she wanted her mother's hand to shake her so she could open her eyes and wake up. She used to be so happy when, as a child, she opened her eyes and realized that the monster which had tried to rip her body to pieces was nothing but a dream, or a nightmare as her mother used to call it. Each time she had opened her eyes, she was very happy to discover that the monster had vanished, that it was only a dream. But now she opened her eyes and the monster did not go away. She opened her eyes and the monster stayed on her body. Her terror was so great that she closed her eyes again to sleep, to make believe that it was a nightmare. But she opened her eyes and knew it was no dream. And she remembered everything.

The first thing she remembered was her mother's scream in the silence of the night. She was sleeping in her mother's arms, like a child of six even though she was an adult and in her twenties. But her mother had said: You'll sleep in my arms so that even if they come in the middle of the night, I will know it and I'll hold on to you with all my might and if they take you they'll have to take me as well.

Nothing was as painful to her as seeing her mother's face move further and further away until it disappeared. Her face, her eyes, her hair, were so pale. She would rather have died than see her mother's face so haggard. To herself she said: Can you forgive me, Mother, for causing you so much pain? Her mother always used to say to her: What's politics got to do with you? You're not a man. Girls of your age think only about marriage. She hadn't replied when her mother had said: Politics is a dirty game which only ineffectual men play.

The voices had now become clearer. The picture also looked clearer, even though the fog was still thick. Was it winter and the hall roofless, or was it summer and they were smoking in a windowless room? She could see another man sitting not far from the judge. His head, like the judge's, was smooth and red but, unlike the judge's, it was not completely under the shoe. He was sitting to one side and above his head hung another picture in which there was something like a flag or a small multicoloured banner. And for the first time, her ears made out some intelligible sentences:

Imagine, ladies and gentlemen. This student, who is not yet twenty years old, refers to Him, whom God protect to lead this noble nation all his life, as 'stupid'.

The word 'stupid' fell like a stone in a sea of awesome silence, making a sound like the crash of a rock in water or the blow of a hand against something solid, like a slap or the clap of one hand against another.

Was someone clapping? She pricked up her ears to catch the sound. Was it applause? Or a burst of laughter, like a cackle? Then that terrifying silence pervaded the courtroom once again, a long silence in which she could hear the beating of her heart. The sound of laughter or of applause echoed in her ears. She asked herself who could be applauding at so serious a moment as when the mighty one was being described as stupid, and aloud too.

Her body was still stuck to the wooden seat, clinging on to it, frightened it would suddenly be taken away. The wound in her lower abdomen was still weeping. But she was able to move her head and half opened her eyes to search for the source of that applause. Suddenly she discovered that the hall was full of heads crammed together in rows, all of them undoubtedly human. Some of the heads appeared to have a lot of hair, as if they were those of women or girls. Some of them were small, as if those of children. One head seemed to be like that of her younger sister. Her body trembled for a moment on the seat as her eyes searched around. Had she come alone or with her father and mother? Were they looking at her now? How did she look? Could they recognize her face or her body?

She turned her head to look. Although her vision had grown weak, she could just make out her mother. She could pick out her mother's face from among thousands of faces even with her eyes closed. Could her mother really be here in the hall? Her heartbeats grew audible and anxiety grew inside her. Anxiety often gripped her and she felt that something terrible had happened to her mother. One night, fear had overcome her when she was curled up like a small animal and she'd told herself: She must have died and I will not see her when I get out. But the following day, she had seen her mother when she came to visit. She'd come, safe and sound. She was happy and said: Don't die, Mother, before I get out and can make up for all the pain I've caused you.

The sound was now clear in her ears. It wasn't just one clap but a whole series of them. The heads in the hall were moving here and there. The judge was still sitting, his smooth head beneath the shoe. The hammer in his hand was moving impatiently, banging rapidly on the wooden table. But the clapping did not stop. The judge rose to his feet so that his head was in the centre of the stomach in the picture. His lower lip trembled as he shouted out words of rebuke which she couldn't hear in all the uproar.

Then silence descended for a period. She was still trying to see, her hands by her side holding on to the seat, clinging on to it, pressing it as if she wanted to confirm that it was really beneath her or that she was really sitting on it. She knew she was awake and not asleep with her eyes closed. Before, when she opened her eyes, the monster would disappear and she'd be happy that it was only a dream. But now she was no longer capable of being happy and had become frightened of opening her eyes.

The noise in the hall had died down and the heads moved as they had done before. All except one head. It was neither smooth nor red. It was covered in a thick mop of white hair and was fixed and immobile. The eyes also did not move and were open, dry and fixed on that small body piled on top of the wooden seat. Her hands were clasped over her chest, her heart under her hand beating fast, her breath panting as if she were running to the end of the track and could no longer breath. Her voice broke as she said to herself: My God! Her eyes turn in my direction but she doesn't see me. What have they done to her eyes? Or is she fighting sleep? God of Heaven and Earth, how could you let them do all that? How, my daugther, did you stand so much pain? How did I stand it together with you? I always felt that you, my daughter, were capable of anything, of moving mountains or of crumbling rocks, even though your body is small and weak like mine. But when your tiny feet used to kick the walls of my stomach, I'd say to myself: God, what strength and power there is inside my body? Your movements were strong while you were still a foetus and shook me from inside, like a volcano shakes the earth. And yet I knew that you were as small as I was, your bones as delicate as your father's, as tall and slim as your grandmother, your feet as large as the feet of prophets. When I gave birth to you, your grandmother pursed her lips in sorrow and said: A girl and ugly too! A double catastrophe! I tensed my stomach muscles to close off my womb to the pain and the blood and, breathing with difficulty, for your birth had been hard and I suffered as though I'd given birth to a mountain, I said to her: She's more precious to me than the whole world! I held you to my breast and slept deeply. Can I, my daughter, again enjoy another moment of deep sleep whilst you are inside me or at least near to me so that I can reach out to touch you? Or whilst you are in your room next to mine so that I can tiptoe in to see you whilst you sleep? The blanket always used to fall off you as you slept, so I'd lift it and cover you. Anxiety would waken me every night and make me creep into your room. What was that anxiety and at what moment did it happen? Was it the moment the cover fell off your body? I could always feel you, even if you had gone away and were out of my sight. Even if they were to bury you under the earth or build a solid wall of mud or iron around you, I would still feel a draught of air on your body as though it were on mine. I sometimes wonder whether I ever really gave birth to you or if you are still inside me. How else could I feel the air when it touches you and hunger when it grips you. Your pain is mine, like fire burning in my breast and stomach. God of Heaven and Earth, how did your body and mine stand it? But I couldn't have stood it were it not for the joy of you being my daughter, of having given birth to you. And you can raise your head high above the moutains of filth. For three thousand and twenty-five hours (I've counted them one by one), they left you with the vomit and pus and the weeping wound in your stomach. I remember the look in your eyes when you told me, the bars between us: If only the weeping were red blood. But it's not red. It's white and has the smell of death. What was it I said to you that day? I don't know, but I said something. I said that the smell becomes normal when we get used to it and live with it every day. I could not look into your emaciated face, but I heard you say: It's not a smell, mother, like other smells which enter through the nose or mouth. It's more like liquid air or steam turned to viscid water or molten lead flowing into every opening of the body. I don't know, mother, if it is burning hot or icy cold. I clasped my hands to my breast, then grasped your slender hand through the bars, saying: When heat become like cold, my daughter, then everything is bearable. But as soon as I left you, I felt my heart swell and swell until it filled my chest and pressed on my lungs so I could no longer breathe. I felt I was choking and tilted my head skywards to force air into my lungs. But the sky that day was void of air and the sun over my head was molten lead like the fire of hell. The eyes of the guards stung me and their uncouth voices piled up inside me. If the earth had transformed into the face of one of them, I'd have spat and spat and spat on it until my throat and chest dried up. Yes, my daughter, brace the muscles of your back and raise your head and turn it in my direction, for I'm sitting near you. You may have heard them when they applauded you. Did you hear them? I saw you move your head towards us. Did you see us? Me and your father and little sister? We all applauded with them. Did you see us?

Her eyes were still trying to penetrate the thick fog. The judge was still standing, his head smooth and red, his lower lip trembling with rapid words. To his right and to his left, she saw smooth red heads begin to move away from that elevated table. The judge's head and the others vanished, although the picture on the wall remained where it was. The face and the eyes were the same as they had been, but now one eye appeared to her to be smaller, as though half-closed or winking at her, that common gesture that a man makes to a woman when he wants to flirt with her. Her body trembled in surprise. Was it possible that he was winking at her? Was it possible for his eyes in the picture to move? Could objects move? Or was she sick and hallucinating? She felt the seat under her palm and raised her hand to touch her body. A fierce heat emanated from it, like a searing flame, a fire within her chest. She wanted to open her mouth and say: Please, a glass of water. But her lips were stuck together, a horizontal line as taut as wire. Her eyes too were stuck on the picture, while the eye in the picture continued to wink at her. Why was it winking at her? Was it flirting with her? She had only discovered that winking was a form of greeting when, two years previously, she'd seen a file of foreign tourists walking in the street. She'd been on her way to the university. Whenever she looked at the faces of one of the men or women, an eye would suddenly wink at her strangely. She had been shocked and hadn't understood how a woman could flirt with her in such a way. Only later had she understood that it was an American form of greeting.

The podium was still empty, without the judge and the smooth heads around him. Silence prevailed. The heads in the hall were still close together in rows and her eyes still roamed in search of a mop of white hair, a pair of black eyes which she could see with eyes closed. But there were so many heads close together she could only see a mound of black and white, circles or squares or oblongs. Her nose began to move as if she were sniffing, for she knew her mother's smell and could distinguish it from thousands of others. It was the smell of milk when she was a child at the breast or the smell of the morning when it rises or the night when it sleeps or the rain on wet earth or the sun above the bed or hot soup in a bowl. She said to herself: Is it possible that you're not here, Mother? And Father, have you come?

The fog before her eyes was still thick. Her head

continued to move in the direction of the rows of crammed heads. The black and white circles were interlocked in tireless movement. Only one circle of black hair was immobile above a wide brown forehead, two firm eyes in a pale slender face and a small body piled on to a chair behind bars. His large gaunt hands gripped his knees, pressing on them from the pain. But the moment he heard the applause, he took his hands off his knees and brought them together to clap. His hands did not return to his knees, the pain in his legs no longer tangible. His heart beat loudly in time to his clapping which shook his slender body on the seat. His eyes began to scour the faces and eyes, and his lips parted a little as though he were about to shout: I'm her father, I'm Al-Fargani who fathered her and whose name she bears. My God, how all the pain in my body vanished in one go with the burst of applause. What if I were to stand up now and reveal my identity to them? This moment is unique and I must not lose it. Men like us live and die for one moment such as this, for others to recognize us, to applaud us, for us to become heroes with eyes looking at us and fingers pointing at us. I have suffered the pain and torture with her, day after day, hour after hour, and now I have the right to enjoy some of the reward and share in her heroism.

He shifted his body slightly on his seat as if he were about to stand up. But he remained seated, though his head still moved. His eyes glanced from face to face, as if he wanted someone to recognize him. The angry voice of the judge and the sharp rapid blows of his hammer on the table broke into the applause. Presently the judge and those with him withdrew to the conference chambers. Silence again descended on the hall, a long and awesome silence, during which some faint whispers reached his ears: They'll cook up the case in the conference chamber . . . That's common pratice . . . Justice and law don't exist here . . . In a while they'll declare the public hearing closed . . . She must be a heroine to have stayed alive until now . . . Imagine that young girl who is sitting in the dock causing the government so much alarm . . . Do you know how they tortured her? Ten men raped her, one after the other. They trampled on her honour and on her father's honour. Her poor father! Do you know him! They say he's ill in bed. Maybe he can't face people after his honour was violated!

At that moment he raised his hands to cover his ears so as not to hear, to press on his head so that it sunk into his chest, pushing it more and more to merge his body into the seat or underneath it or under the ground. He wanted to vanish so that no one would see or know him. His name was not Al-Fargani, not Assharqawi, not Azziftawi, not anything. He had neither name nor existence. What is left of a man whose honour is violated? He had told her bitterly: Politics, my girl, is not for women and girls. But she had not listened to him. If she had been a man, he would not be suffering now the way he was. None of those dogs would have been able to violate his honour and dignity. Death was preferable for him and for her now.

Silence still reigned over the hall. The judge and his entourage had not yet reappeared. Her eyes kept trying to see, searching out one face amongst the faces, for eyes she recognized, for a mop of white hair the colour of children's milk. But all she could see were black and white circles and squares inter-mingled and constantly moving. Is it possible you're not here, Mother? Is Father still ill? Her nose too continued to move here and there, searching for a familiar smell, the smell of a warm breast full of milk, the smell of the sun and of drizzle on grass. But her nose was unable to pick up the smell. All it could pick up was the smell of her body crumpled on the seat and the weeping wound between her thighs. It was a smell of pus and blood and the putrid stench of the breath and sweat of ten men, the marks of whose nails were still on her body, with their uncouth voices, their saliva and the sound of their snorting. One of them, lying on top of her, had said: This is the way we torture you women — by depriving you of the most valuable thing you possess. Her body under him was as cold as a corpse but she had managed to open her mouth and say to him: You fool! The most valuable thing I possess is not between my legs. You're all stupid. And the most stupid among you is the one who leads you.

She craned her neck to raise her head and penetrate the fog with her weak eyes. The many heads were still crammed together and her eyes still strained. If only she could have seen her mother for a moment, or her father or little sister, she would have told them something strange. She would have told them that they had stopped using that method of torture when they discovered that it didn't torture her. They began to search for other methods.

In the conference chamber next to the hall, the judge and his aides were meeting, deliberating the case. What should they do now that the public had applauded the accused? The judge began to face accusations in his turn:

— We're not accusing you, Your Honour, but you did embarrass us all. As the saying goes: 'The road to hell is paved with good intentions'! You did what you thought was right, but you only managed to make things worse. How could you say, Your Honour, about Him, whom God protect to lead this noble nation all his life, that he is stupid?

— God forbid, sir! I didn't say that, I said that *she* said he was stupid.

— Don't you know the saying, 'What the ear doesn't hear, the heart doesn't grieve over'? You declared in public that he's stupid.

— I didn't say it, sir. I merely repeated what the accused said to make the accusation stick. That's precisely what my job is.

— Yes, that's your job, Your Honour. We know that. But you should have been smarter and wiser than that.

— I don't understand.

— Didn't you hear how the people applauded her?

— Is that my fault?

— Don't you know why they applauded?

— No, I don't.

— Because you said in public what is said in private and it was more like confirming a fact than proving an accusation.

— What else could I have done, sir?

— You could have said that she cursed the mighty one without saying exactly *what* she said.

— And if I'd been asked what kind of curse it was?

— Nobody would have asked you. And besides, you volunteered the answer before anyone asked, as though you'd seized the opportunity to say aloud and in her words, what you yourself wanted to say or perhaps what you do say to yourself in secret.

— Me? How can you accuse me in this way? I was simply performing my duty as I should. Nobody can accuse me of anything. Perhaps I was foolish, but you cannot accuse me of bad faith.

— But foolishness can sometimes be worse than bad faith. You must know that foolishness is the worst label you can stick on a man. And as far as he's concerned, better that he be a swindler, a liar, a miser, a trickster, even a thief or a traitor, rather than foolish. Foolishness means that he doesn't think, that he's mindless, that he's an animal. That's the worst thing you can call an ordinary man. And all the more so if he's a ruler. You don't know rulers, Your Honour, but I know them well. Each of them fancies his brain to be better than any other man's. And it's not just a matter of fantasy, but of blind belief, like the belief in God. For the sake of this illusion, he can kill thousands.

— I didn't know that, sir. How can I get out of this predicament?

— I don't know why you began with the description 'stupid', Your Honour. If you'd read everything she said, you'd have found that she used other less ugly terms to describe him.

— Such as what, sir? Please, use your experience to help me choose some of them. I don't want to leave here accused, after coming in this morning to raise an accusation.

— Such descriptions cannot be voiced in public. The session must be closed. Even a less ugly description will find an echo in the heart of the people if openly declared. That's what closed sessions are for, Your Honour. Many matters escape you and it seems you have little experience in law.

A few minutes later, utter silence descended on the hall. The courtroom was completely emptied. As for her, they took her back to where she'd been before.

A Private Letter
to an Artist Friend

A Private Letter
to an Artist Friend

Since you opened your heart to me and reproached me sternly yet gently, the gentleness making me cry more than the sternness, since you did that, I now have the right to reproach you, as one artist to another, as a woman to a man between whom the feeling of closeness is firm and deep-rooted and as translucent as pure air. But although we feel it to be deep and almost filling us, we are incapable of holding on to it in a moment of reality. And it seems that this is the only characteristic of feelings of closeness, that in so far as they are real they seem to us like a dream.

Since you did that, allow me to reproach you. I have never reproached anyone before. I never reproached my father or my mother for bringing me into this world without consulting me; neither will I reproach God for taking me without my volition. No, I reproach no one, neither man nor woman nor God, neither in love nor in hatred. And how much more harm I've suffered through love than through hatred!

But you have become one of those rare and exceptional people in my life. And when I pick up my pen, what I write is not for people in general to read but rather for one particular person, for him alone to read, separate from all the rest.

At times, even if I try, I find myself unable to write deep and very personal things for myself, as though there were some deep-seated wound, some bottomless well into which I have fallen. And I feel the pain in my skull reach to the very core. Is it my destiny to be something other than what destiny decreed for me? Not to be female (in the accepted sense of the word) and not to be a doctor (according to my degree from medical school)? Or is it really my destiny to be a person before being a female, an artist before being a doctor?

Ever since I was born I have felt my struggle to be with destiny itself, although another side of me realizes that destiny is with me, that it is destiny that wants me to be an artist and a person. What, then, is that other force that wants me to be a female and a doctor? Is there any destiny other than the destiny we know?

All my life I have been torn between two destinies, like a piece of meat held between predatory jaws. I try to run away and sometimes I believe I have managed to escape, that I am spared. I take a deep breath and pick up a pen to pour myself on to paper, truthfully, as naturally as death, as simply as a spontaneous smile on the face of a child. And with the naïveté of a child, I believe I have done nothing worthwhile. Even as the words on the page seem to me inadequate, less and weaker than myself, the world around me quakes in fear, as though honesty were no longer a word but a beast of prey, as though truth had become like death or worse.

And is there anything worse than death? Or perhaps it is our lives which, at times, become worse than death. I used to ask myself this question, but I don't know if there is an answer, in life or in death. Most of the time, I don't know the difference between living and dying. At times, my life seems to me like death, whilst at others, death suddenly appears to me to be the only hope for living.

A deep pain reaches deeper than any knife can. I look around me, searching for others like me who carry knives in their bodies, looking for another person who can tell me, 'Yes, you're in the right and the world is in the wrong. You tell the truth and the world tells lies.'

But such people are very rare, as rare as a truthful word lost between heaven and earth like a drop of water lost in the sea, like an honest heartbeat lost inside the breast and which not one of us can find even if we wanted to. How often, amongst the millions of heartbeats, is there a real one? Every minute the heart beats about seventy times, four thousand times an hour, three million times a month. How often does the heart beat in a lifetime? Do any of us recognize a true heartbeat amongst the millions? And even if we did recognize it, could we grasp it, if we wanted to?

Contrary to what they taught me, I realized that the sum of my life did not amount to the number of years between the date of my birth and my death. I realized for certain that there is a heartbeat other than that of the heart and that the sum total of my whole life may be the one true heartbeat I manage to grasp amongst the millions of untrue ones, or a spontaneous truthful word which I manage to capture on a page amongst the millions of un-spontaneous words.

I realized this truth for certain. I realized it with my mind and body, with both together, and with all my senses. And yet, how often did this extraordinary certainty turn, at times, into extraordinary doubt, which itself became certainty and whilst anything else became doubt. At such times, I feel as if I have been slaughtered, physically and mentally, that I am in the wrong and that it is the world which is right. I may see myself walking in the street or driving my car, but I know for certain that I have been slaughtered, that the body which is moving is not my real body, that the murderers have hidden my body in a hole in the ground. And I see my unreal body move before me. It may shake hands with people. It may smile. It may pretend and tell the world it is right and I am wrong. . . .

How did I pull my slaughtered body from out of the ground? How did I force my semi-paralysed hand to hold a pen? I don't know, but at any given moment, when I may be sitting or standing or driving, alone or with other people, I see my body rise of its own accord and find myself standing when I was sitting, or sitting when I was standing, or running away from people when I was with them or running towards people when I was alone.

With a shudder of fear, like one coming face to face with death, I discover to my great surprise that my body is really trembling, that my voice trembles. But it lasts only for a fleeting moment, like a single cry which I may hurl in the face of a speaker to silence him or in the face of a silent person to make him speak.

In one such moment, the speaker was an important man, my supervisor in my medical work. He was one of those men of whom the world is full: a doctor who measures his medical achievements by the area of land he owns in this world; a man like the males of the world, who know women only as females. He wanted to treat me like he treats the rest of the world, but I refused. Refusal for me was easy and natural, since I am a person by nature and not a female. And I am by nature an artist and not a doctor. Refusal for me is as easy and natural as the air I breathe. But for him, refusal was hard, harder than death.

It has always puzzled me why men are unable to cope with refusal, especially the refusal of a woman. I see the face of one of them, from which the blood ebbs away until it becomes as white as death. Does this refusal expose his real face to himself, so that he realizes for the first time that it is a dead face? Or that he is refused within himself as well and is suddenly unable to cope with both refusals together?

In an authoritarian tone he told me that no employee ever argued with him, that no woman had ever defied him before. He opened the drawer of his luxurious desk and took out certificates testifying to his superiority and heroism and his victory medals. The walls of his room were plastered with golden frames containing certificates from Egypt and abroad. The blood returned to his face and it was no longer white. His head was held high above a short neck bound by a large necktie (in the American fashion) and his chest was puffed out by tense back muscles which he held with difficulty and effort as if he were unable to convince his own body muscles of his numerous external achievements, as if internally he were defeated by a failure of which no one knew.

Perhaps he saw or felt that I was the only one who witnessed his failure. And because I was a woman, his failure was compounded. His pleasure turned to anger, his approval to disapproval. The desire to nominate me for promotion and to raise me up to seventh heaven turned into the desire to bury me in the heart of the earth and to close the hole with sealing wax.

It was not the first time I'd witnessed a man's failure. There are many men but the number of failures is greater and in the end, I was only one woman. But despite being a woman, despite being only one woman, I had realized that amongst the multitude of men there was at least one who was not defeated. I realized that with every step I took, with every movement or turn I made, be it merely a momentary head movement walking down some street or other, whether consciously or unconsciously, willingly or unwillingly, with mind or body or both together, I realized that I was searching for that man. I also realized that he was not the only man, that there were maybe two or three or four, maybe no more than could be counted on the fingers of one hand, but they were there, albeit rare, and as long as they were there, I had to search for them.

I noticed you once, when I was walking at my normal fast pace. I was angry with that supervisor and when I'm angry I begin to walk faster. Anger shows me heading for a new battle. I must not waste time along the way, each second of my life becomes valuable and the feeling of time passing becomes so oppressive that I must run, scared that death will catch up with me before I can enter into combat, as though it is the last battle of my life and after it I will die. But since I am basically dead, I'm not afraid of death. And because I don't fear death, people are afraid of me. That is the only reason that I come out alive from every battle and remain on earth.

That day you asked me about my anger, so I told you. I hadn't told anyone before and didn't know what to say. Even if I had known, I wouldn't have been able to speak, for there was nobody to hear me or to believe me had I spoken. And what could I have said? That the whole world was in the wrong and I alone was in the right? That the world was mad and I alone was sane? That since the time I was born I have felt letters coursing through my veins like the circulation of blood? That when I hold a pen, the whole world disappears along with the pleasures of food and love and sex and death? That I vanish into a sentence like one lost to love or death? And yet, despite all that, I realize that I'm not lost to anything. Can I say that art was my choice and will but that I am female by chance? That since childhood I have rejected my femininity because it was not me, not of my making, but rather that of a world full of masculinity but void of men? Can I say that I tackle my life with little intellect but with a lot of love? That I do not praise the intellect, despite my medical diplomas, since it's the world around us which moulds our intellects? And because the world is false, it has made our intellects false. In our revolution against the world, we must revolt against our own intellects. Can I say all this? And if I were to say it, would anyone believe me?

That day you told me you believed me. I was so surprised that I couldn't believe it. I sat transfixed in my chair before you. I wanted to stay a while but I got up and left. I don't remember why I left. Maybe someone came in, maybe the phone or door bell rang. What matters is that I left and that we've met only rarely since that day. Sometimes I catch sight of you walking fast in the street, while I too am walking fast. Sometimes I notice something you've written and I stop and remember. Or sometimes I notice your face in a sea of faces and I look up and wave to you from afar if you've seen me. If you don't see me, I turn around and walk away quickly. And despite my rapid steps, I used to feel as though something of you was with me for ever. I ask myself whether you too feel that I gave you something of myself in a moment which has passed and which I cannot retrieve. Sometimes I'd get into my car to come to you but I'd stop myself and wonder what I'd say to you. Whether you remembered what happened between us. Whether something really happened for you to remember.

I don't know if something happened. If it did, what was it? Was it something that the memory can hold on to as proof? Something which could justify my going to you, were I to go? One reason I could put into words were you to ask me why I'd come?

How many years passed without my going to you? I don't know. I don't measure time in terms of years. My whole life, in my view, may not be equal to one moment which I feel with my mind and body and with all my reserve energy. I have always realized that the senses I have are not all I have, that under the surface is a pulse other than that of the heart, another mind under the mind, another body under the body. Is there another whole woman inside? And which of them is me? Which is real and which unreal? I have always felt that there is only a hair's breadth between the real and unreal and I continually try to cross it to reach the unknown. Both the known and the unknown I feel like fear inside my body. Medicine and surgery have broken the fear of the body, in my view, and art the fear of the unknown. I allowed myself to talk about all the parts of the body like poets talk of the beating of the heart. And I always ask myself why the beat of the heart is the only one permitted.

How many years passed without me coming to you? I don't remember. But I do remember that once, on the spur of the moment, in one of those leaps when I cross that hair's breadth between the known and unknown, between certainty and doubt, when I realize that the world is in the wrong and I am in the right and I break out of my life like one possessed by the sudden desire for death, or I

107

break out of my death in the sudden hope for life – in one of those moments I reached for the telephone and called your number. A man's voice replied and said that you weren't there, so I left my name and number and said I was waiting for your reply.

How many years did I wait? I don't remember and did not try to remember. I grew sad and the sadness erased my memory so that I no longer remembered. Each time I did remember, I grew sadder and forgot until I was sad no longer and no longer forgot. And on the occasions when I almost did remember, I did not know exactly what there was to remember. Nothing had happened between us that the memory could hold on to and there was no proof, no reason, no justification which I could speak of, had someone asked me.

Once I noticed you from afar and I stopped and moved in your direction. But then I turned around and walked away quickly, asking myself if it was love or not. Have things got so complicated? To the extent of being unable to distinguish love from lack of love, to see white from black? Like a blind person, I stood still for a moment to hold my head in my hands and close my eyes or open them. I asked myself if the world had stolen the sight from my eyes, if the world had fragmented the nerves of the eye and heart.

I realized that the world had fragmented everything, fragmented humanity into master and slave, fragmented the individual into mind and body, the body into reputable and disreputable parts. I realized that the world had fragmented everything, apart from myself. Had fragmented men, women, children, rulers and ruled. There is nothing separating political fragmentation from sexual fragmentation. The truthful artist falls with his truthfulness into the game of politics and drowns with his art in the snares of sex. Both politics and sex are the adversaries of art and of humanity. But the artist who, through his art, is committed to the ranks of the ruled in any name or land; who, through his humanity, rejects the body of the rulers in any shape or form; who, by his view, is attracted to sex under the illusion of any love; who is committed to the world with everything in it and on it, while knowing for certain that the world will fragment him, is just as certain that he will never be fragmented.

How many years passed without me going to you? Once I happened to open a newspaper, even though I never look at papers in a world in which pens and bodies tell lies. But that morning, for some reason, I picked up a paper. Perhaps I intended to line a kitchen shelf with it, but I noticed your face and read your careful black words. The printed letters looked almost like your handwriting. The truthfulness of the words on the page had a movement which resembled the movement of your eyes when they look at me. Did you see me in front of you as you wrote? But you haven't seen me for many a long year and no memory, however powerful, can retain something that happened many years ago, let alone something that did *not* happen.

When the phone rang, I believed it came from anywhere in the world but your office. When I came to you, I thought we would exchange some commonplace words, like those accepted courtesies between acquaintances and friends. But your words were not commonplace and your reproach was not commonplace. In as much as I was surprised, I was not surprised. In as much as I was hurt, I was not hurt. I told you that I had tried once to contact you but had got no reply. You did not believe me and told me that if I'd wanted to come, I would have come. I insisted that I had tried, but you did not believe me and told me that had I really wanted to get in touch with you, nothing could have prevented our meeting. You were very harsh in not believing me. The more your harshness hurt me, the more surprised I was. Perhaps you saw the surprise in my eyes resembling tears. I was so surprised I almost did cry. After all these years, can the memory retain something that did not happen? Or if it did happen, was only for a brief moment, like a flash of light which appears and then vanishes, like the heartbeat which beats once, then falls into oblivion amongst the millions of others.

When you took my hand in yours to say goodbye, I knew you would kiss me and that your kiss on my face would be tender and delicate, almost translucent, like the kiss of a child kissing another, innocent and yet not innocent, like all instinctive feelings.

You gave me your phone number on a scrap of paper and I promised you I'd phone. I was sincere in my promise but as soon as I went out into the crowded street, everything seemed to me like a dream or an illusion. The reproach seemed to be something normal which can happen between any two friends meeting after a long separation. The kiss also seemed normal between friends or colleagues.

110

And, walking at my rapid pace, I realized I would continue walking at my usual speed until I died walking, that many more long years would pass before I could distinguish the real from the unreal, that I was incapable of defying death, unable to cross that hair's breadth between doubt and certainty. Am I in the right and the world in the wrong? Or am I in the wrong and the world right? If you did not believe me that time, I reproach you. If you did believe me, my reproach of you is all the stronger.

A Selected List of Titles Available from Minerva

While every effort is made to keep prices low, it is sometimes necessary to increase prices at short notice. Mandarin Paperbacks reserves the right to show new retail prices on covers which may differ from those previously advertised in the text or elsewhere.

The prices shown below were correct at the time of going to press.

Fiction
☐	7493 9026 3	**I Pass Like Night**	Jonathan Ames	£3.99 BX
☐	7493 9006 9	**The Tidewater Tales**	John Bath	£4.99 BX
☐	7493 9004 2	**A Casual Brutality**	Neil Blessondath	£4.50 BX
☐	7493 9028 2	**Interior**	Justin Cartwright	£3.99 BC
☐	7493 9002 6	**No Telephone to Heaven**	Michelle Cliff	£3.99 BX
☐	7493 9028 X	**Not Not While the Giro**	James Kelman	£4.50 BX
☐	7493 9011 5	**Parable of the Blind**	Gert Hofmann	£3.99 BC
☐	7493 9010 7	**The Inventor**	Jakov Lind	£3.99 BC
☐	7493 9003 4	**Fall of the Imam**	Nawal El Saadewi	£3.99 BC

Non-Fiction
☐	7493 9012 3	**Days in the Life**	Jonathon Green	£4.99 BC
☐	7493 9019 0	**In Search of J D Salinger**	Ian Hamilton	£4.99 BX
☐	7493 9023 9	**Stealing from a Deep Place**	Brian Hall	£3.99 BX
☐	7493 9005 0	**The Orton Diaries**	John Lahr	£5.99 BC
☐	7493 9014 X	**Nora**	Brenda Maddox	£6.99 BC

All these books are available at your bookshop or newsagent, or can be ordered direct from the publisher. Just tick the titles you want and fill in the form below. Available in:
BX: British Commonwealth excluding Canada
BC: British Commonwealth including Canada

Mandarin Paperbacks, Cash Sales Department, PO Box 11, Falmouth, Cornwall TR10 9EN.

Please send cheque or postal order, no currency, for purchase price quoted and allow the following for postage and packing:

UK	80p for the first book, 20p for each additional book ordered to a maximum charge of £2.00.
BFPO	80p for the first book, 20p for each additional book.
Overseas including Eire	£1.50 for the first book, £1.00 for the second and 30p for each additional book thereafter.

NAME (Block letters) ....

ADDRESS ....

....

....